Epilogue II
One American's
OPINION

EPILOGUE II
ONE AMERICAN'S
OPINION

FOR PATRIOTS WHO LOVE THEIR COUNTRY

R. LYNN WILSON

iUniverse

EPILOGUE II ONE AMERICAN'S OPINION
FOR PATRIOTS WHO LOVE THEIR COUNTRY

iUniverse books may be ordered through booksellers or by contacting:

iUniverse
1663 Liberty Drive
Bloomington, IN 47403
www.iuniverse.com
1-800-Authors (1-800-288-4677)

ISBN: 978-1-5320-4101-3 (sc)
ISBN: 978-1-5320-4100-6 (e)

Library of Congress Control Number: 2018900261

Print information available on the last page.

iUniverse rev. date: 02/07/2018

PREFACE

Epilogue II is written to summarize and update the book I published in 2016 titled *One American's Opinion: For Patriots Who Love Their Country*. As the original book, Epilogue II is written from the acquired knowledge in my head, copious ardent research, and the intrinsic values in my heart to reflect my dyed-in-the-wool conservative soul and my enormous love for our country. It is that soul and love that provided the motivation to commit the time and energy to author the original book and Epilogue II.

The original book was intended to be a one-year project to offer my observations and opinion on the 2014 midterm national election. One year turned into three years as I discovered through my research the true intent of the progressive movement in America. That true intent is to replace our traditional American values that have made our country the greatest society in history with Marxist ideology. I was also taken aback by how invasive Marxist-based progressivism had become in the functioning of local, state, and federal governments and the impact that is having on American society. Based upon what I learned, the original book's focus changed from an election to an in-depth look at our country's future based on that impact.

Epilogue II was intended to update the material contained in the original book and to analyze President Trump's first few months in office. I had intended to do that by republishing the original book and replacing the original epilogue with this one. However, like the original book, Epilogue II became a much bigger project after I discovered through Trump's presidency how pervasive progressives have become in American society through known and unknown Marxist-based organizations and how diabolical and successful progressives have been in developing a federal shadow government or, as many call it, the deep state. A two or three-month project became a twelve-month project and resulted in this supplemental book to the original.

As with the original book, one of the biggest problems I experienced was keeping Epilogue II's content current over the twelve-month period. Many of the events I used to support my premises are still ongoing. I constantly updated information until the book went to press. The whole book was in perpetual motion as I wrote. I am sure by the time you read this; you will find outdated information but that in no way changes the salient points made, my opinions, or the book's final premise.

I am a very patriotic and proud American. We are so extraordinarily lucky to live in the most wonderful and successful country in the history of the Earth in terms of economic opportunity, standard of living, personal freedom, and personal safety. I cannot sit back and do nothing to counter the progressives who want to take that away from us for their own demented and nefarious purposes. My original book, Epilogue II, my guest editorials in the local newspaper, monetary contributions to conservative organizations, ranting with my conservative family and friends, expressing my support for traditional American values to politicians and others, and my well-informed vote in every election are my contributions to that end.

Our country is at a crossroads for its future—more so than I realized when I wrote the original book. Unless our American society takes a strong stand to return to our traditional roots, America is doomed to no longer have the distinction of being the most wonderful and successful country in the history of the Earth. There are those Americans who won't know the difference and those of us who will feel great sadness for our current family, family generations to come, and even those Americans who are clueless. I sincerely hope Epilogue II will provide motivation for you to boldly stand up for the future of the America that we all love and offers us so much.

All chapter references refer to chapters in the original book. The vast number and variety of sources I used to support and enhance my opinions were not practical to include in a standard bibliography and standard reference footnotes. I did identify references in the text when

I used specific sources to make or support a point in order to give the reference credit, to provide validation for my supporting information, and to allow the reader to research the reference and learn more if they wish. All references to specific months are during 2017 unless otherwise specified. The primary sources for my reference material were: Fox News; The Naples Daily News; The Wall Street Journal; The Heritage Foundation; The Daily Signal (which is the multimedia news organization of The Heritage Foundation); Judicial Watch; conservative and liberal Internet websites; Internet websites for national newspapers; and Wikipedia.

EPILOGUE II

George Orwell once described writing a book as "a horrible, exhausting struggle like a long bout of some painful illness". Best selling American author, Daniel Silva, said in his book titled *The Secret Servant* that he neglected to mention the only people who suffer more than the writer himself are the loved ones forced to live with him. My wonderful wife can attest to that. I finished the original book in July 2016 and here I am in 2017 writing Epilogue II.

Donald Trump has been our president since January 20th. I am sitting here pondering what I should write regarding the impact President Trump will have on my prediction in chapter 13 for the future of America. I'm going to start by repeating what I wrote in the first Epilogue. If the winner had been Hillary Clinton, I know exactly what I would write. I would paraphrase a comment by Eric Bolling when he was on Fox News' *The Five*. He said, "Behind Hillary's door, we know there is certain death (for America) but behind Trump's door, we have a 50/50 chance." Let's look at that in more detail. Edward Klein wrote in his book titled *Guilty As Sin* that a Hillary Clinton presidency would result in:

- More taxpayer-financed "free stuff" for favored Democratic groups
- More national debt
- More business regulations
- More government-directed crony capitalism
- More layoffs
- More unconstitutional executive orders
- More politics of envy

- More illegal immigrants
- More Islamic terrorism
- More Clinton scandals
- More favors for big-bucks contributions
- More gridlock in Washington
- More division between blacks and whites
- More criticism of the police and more crime and disorder
- More Obamacare and higher premiums
- More downsizing of the armed forces
- More late-term abortions
- More out-of-wedlock children supported by welfare
- More gun control
- More federal control of public schools
- More "multi-gender" bathrooms
- More liberal Supreme Court Justices
- More political correctness
- More assaults on free speech on college campuses
- More chaos in the Middle East
- More humiliation from China, Russia, and Iran
- More, in other words, of the last eight years under President Obama

As I read this list, it sounds like a summary of the original book. A Hillary Clinton presidency would have been a continuation of the Obama administration with unbridled personal corruption thrown in. Speaking of unbridled personal corruption, I decided to research Hillary's personality traits like I did Obama's. I concluded that she exhibits personality traits associated with antisocial personality disorder. The Mayo Clinic provides the following definition:

- Disregard for right or wrong
- Persistent lying or deceit
- Being callous, cynical, and disrespectful of others
- Using charm or wit to manipulate others for personal gain or personal pleasure

- Arrogance, a sense of superiority and being extremely opinioned
- Recurring problems with the law, including criminal behavior
- Repeatedly violating the rights of others through intimidation and dishonesty
- Impulsiveness or failure to plan ahead
- Hostility, significant irritability, agitation, aggression or violence
- Lack of empathy for others and lack of remorse about harming others
- Unnecessary risk-taking or dangerous behavior with no regard for the safety of self or others
- Poor or abusive relationships
- Failure to consider the negative consequences of behavior or learn from them
- Being consistently irresponsible and repeatedly failing to fulfill work or financial obligations

The Mayo Clinic website also said inherited genes could make someone vulnerable to this disorder and being subjected to abuse, neglect, and an unstable life during childhood are risk factors. I have read Edward Klein's books regarding Hillary Clinton titled *Blood Feud*, *Unlikeable*, and *Guilty As Sin*. Klein's writings about Hillary fit these traits and risk factors to a T. This provides an explanation as to how she could lie to the families of those who were killed in Benghazi and then lie that she didn't lie. As I did with Obama, I went to the Internet to see if anyone else shared my opinion. The Internet was full of opinions that Hillary suffered from antisocial personality disorder.

Anyone who runs for president has to be a little crazy, right? Well, I wouldn't go that far but I would say that it takes someone with a strong ego and a good dose of narcissism to have the motivation to run for president, go through what it takes to win the presidency, and then do the job. How about Donald Trump? He also has a major dose of ego and narcissism like Hillary but there is a major difference between Trump, Hillary, and Obama. I surmised in chapter 7 that the ego and narcissism exhibited by Obama results from psychotic based behavior. I surmise the same for Hillary. If you remember, psychotic behavior results in the mental inability to accept that you are ever wrong and a lack of empathy for others.

I believe Trump's ego and narcissism is neurotic based behavior; therefore, he can accept that he can be wrong and does have empathy for others. This conclusion is very significant when judging Trump's ability to be an effective president. Trump showed his outrageous ego and narcissistic side in spades during his campaign and continues to do so as president. Although Trump's behavior probably got him the republican nomination, it was not presidential in the traditional sense and almost cost him the presidential election by giving the Hillary Clinton campaign organization and the news media great fodder to discredit him as presidential material. In reality; however, Trump's ego and narcissism could actually be the catalyst to make him a strong and effective president. It will motivate him to want to go down in history as being admired and successful.

I do wonder sometimes if he ever has second thoughts about becoming president when I see the unwarranted turmoil he and his family have to go through. This reminds me of a great quote by Abraham Lincoln. Lincoln said, "Nearly all men can stand adversity, but if you want to test a man's character, give him power." Time will tell regarding President Trump.

Trump is neither a republican nor a democrat. He is an opportunist who used the republican ticket to win the presidency. He does; however, exhibit strong conservative beliefs and behaviors. Even though the republican ticket won the presidency and kept the House and the Senate, the Republican Party continues to be in a state of disorganization and lacks ideological unity as I discussed in chapter 12. The replacement and repeal debacle regarding Obamacare is a great example.

The lack of unity and support by republican politicians for Trump's conservative agenda is forcing Trump to act unilaterally and attempt to engage democratic political leaders in his effort to get his agenda accomplished. It is no surprise that his attempts so far have fallen on deaf ears. Trump said he was going to "drain the swamp" and we are seeing efforts to do so. It is certainly a messy and difficult process. His mind-set as a corporate business owner working to get things done and not as a politician covering their political ass is obvious. There was an excellent September editorial in The Wall Street Journal by Gerald Seib that discussed this issue. Seib said Trump is probably on safe ground working with democratic leaders because four out of ten Trump supporters said a primary reason they voted for him was to change business as usual in Washington versus only one out of ten wanting him to pursue traditional republican policies.

Can Trump be a president who will bring America back to its traditional roots and save us from the eventual progressive Marxist destruction that I predicted in chapter 13? With that question in mind, let's look into the Trump presidency.

It has been just over ten months since Donald Trump was inaugurated as our 45th president and what a ride during those ten months. Not because of actions by President Trump but because of the onslaught against the Trump administration by an extremely malicious shadow government (also referred to as the deep state) consisting of Obama leftovers in the federal government, the multitude of radical progressive organizations that exist in our country, radical progressive individuals like George Soros, progressive Washington politicians, other progressive politicians across the country, and Obama himself.

You probably know that Valarie Jarrett moved into the Obama household in Washington, D.C. after Trump took office. You and I both know she was not homeless. Oh, and we must not forget the mainstream news media that is being strung along like puppets on a string as a mouthpiece for this crusade.

I am sure you saw the news reports regarding the disruptive attendees at republican congressional town hall meetings after the presidential election. Did you notice all the professionally made signs and observe how the disruption by the majority of those in attendance appeared to be organized? There is a reason for that. It was organized.

My wife and I attended an Americans for Prosperity educational meeting here in Naples to see an old documentary film featuring Saul Alinsky and his community organizing tactics. The documentary was very interesting to say the least and hit home regarding all the organized disruption at republican town hall meetings. We met a couple at the educational meeting who had attended a republican congressman's town hall meeting in Tampa. They told us they arrived at the meeting two or three hours early and the room was packed with organized antagonists who had been bussed to Tampa from the northeastern part of the U.S. They were very unruly during the meeting.

The disruptive behavior at these meetings became so bad that some republican politicians no longer have open meetings and have found other ways to communicate with their constituencies. I don't blame them. It is very sad but not surprising. Progressive organizers turned republican town hall meetings into contrived political slugfests and robbed legitimate constituents of the ability to have open meetings with their political representatives.

Disruptive organizing activity started before the election. I'm sure you remember the demonstrators who were sometimes violent to Trump supporters at Trump's campaign rallies. It has been reliably reported that the organizers of these demonstrations were Hillary Clinton campaign operatives who are well known for their expertise and aggressiveness in political smear tactics and dirty tricks. The violence toward Trump supporters was to create a sense of anarchy associated with Trump. I presume the demonstrators were paid.

How about the disruptive rudeness toward Secretary of Education Betsy DeVos when she gave the commencement address this year at predominately black Bethune-Cookman University? It was reported that the NAACP and the National Education Association teachers' union in Florida orchestrated it, not the students. Organized protests orchestrated by progressive organizations and progressive individuals have become commonplace to associate chaos and negativity with Trump in an effort to discredit him as being legitimate.

A February op-ed in the New York Post by Paul Sperry spoke to this behavior against Trump and his agenda. Sperry is a conservative author, political commentator, and media fellow at the Hoover Institution. The op-ed said Obama has set up a shadow White House in his residence only two miles from the real White House. I wonder if this has anything to do with Valarie Jarrett moving in? Obama was quoted in the op-ed as making the following comments to his aides and old campaign workers before he left office, "But get over it … move forward to protect what we have accomplished. … Now is the time for some organizing, so don't mope."

Obama's re-election campaign in 2012 resulted in an organization titled Organizing for Action (OFA). According to the OFA's Internal Revenue Service (IRS) filings, it is a (501)(c)(4) organization with 32,525 volunteers and has raised more than $40 million since 2013. The filing also says OFA trains "young activists" to develop organizing skills. I read the following statements on their website:

- Your voice can change a room. We respect. We empower. We include. We act.
- OFA is committed to mobilizing and training the next generation of progressive organizers and leaders, because real, lasting change doesn't just happen on its own—it requires a program, it requires organizing, and it requires people like you.
- With grassroots chapters in neighborhoods across the country, OFA volunteers are building this movement from the ground up, person to person, community by community—because democracy isn't a spectator sport.
- Join this fight. The movement needs you now more than ever. Join a long line of progressive organizers.

Sperry said OFA has over 250 offices across the country and is growing. Obama was quoted telling the organization after the election, "You're going to see me early next year and we're going to be in a position where we can start cooking up all kinds of great stuff. … Point is, I'm still fired up and ready to go."

I expressed my great respect for Cal Thomas in the original book. He wrote, "… Barack Obama's Organizing for America appears to operate only to cause harm to and ultimately impeach President Donald Trump. The Saul Alinsky playbook remains the bible of the political left. Obama and Hillary Clinton are, and have long been, Alinsky disciples."

This progressive onslaught is not just an affront against Trump and his administration but against America itself. One can understand progressives being upset at Trump because he won the presidential election and they lost. But why the out of control, vitriolic actions to destroy Trump when at the same time their actions are destructive to our country? The answer is that getting back at Trump is not the true reason for their actions. The true reason is to stop the Trump administration from nullifying the ideological progress made during Obama's eight year reign and continue their advancement of their Marxist-based progressive ideology.

They want to continue their success in accomplishing their dastardly deed of turning America into a Marxist-based society by retaking the House, the Senate, and the presidency in the 2018 midterm and the 2020 presidential elections. I wrote about my research regarding Obama's family, his childhood, and his adulthood in chapter 7. Because of that research, I am convinced that Obama's true political ideology is Marxist-based communism. That opinion is supported by his dictatorial-based behavior during his presidency and his administration's rampant implementation of Marxist-based policies and regulations. I have often wondered how despotic the behavior of a progressive like Obama would become if we did not have term limits for the office of president? Neither Obama nor his progressive colleagues would ever acknowledge their push for a Marxist America.

This Epilogue scrutinizes the progressives' post Obama behavior and its impact on my prophesy for the future of America as spelled out in chapter 13. It also serves as an updated summary of the original book. I quickly learned that I am having the same trouble keeping this Epilogue current as I did the original book. That does not; however, diminish the message this Epilogue delivers regarding an in-depth understanding of what is happening to our country after Trump's election and what that means for America's future.

Let's begin that discussion by revisiting the principles of traditional American values as discussed in chapters 1 and 13 and how they conflict with Marxist-based progressive values. The original colonists came to America to escape religious persecution, escape repression, and to find better economic opportunity. America can only remain America by preserving the colonists' pioneer spirit of personal struggle, hard work, sacrifice, and the love and respect of their fellow man. That pioneer heritage is the basis of the principles and laws set forth in the Declaration of Independence and the Constitution, which provide our American society's foundational structure. I am always amazed at the genius of the governance ideology that went into these founding documents that were written over 240 and 230 years ago respectively.

The Declaration of Independence says, "We hold these truths to be self-evident, that all men are created equal, that they are endowed by their Creator with certain unalienable Rights, that among these are Life, Liberty and the pursuit of Happiness." The Constitution says, "WE THE PEOPLE of the United States, in Order to form a more perfect Union, establish Justice, insure domestic Tranquility, provide for the common defense, promote the general Welfare, and secure the Blessings of Liberty to ourselves and our Posterity, do ordain and establish this Constitution for the United States of America."

Nowhere in either of these founding documents does it say our American society should be for the collective good of the people and be governed in a utopian totalitarian manner—Marxism. Our founding documents say that our society is based upon individual achievement and that every member of our society has the equal right and opportunity to achieve what he or she desires in life. Our cultural heritage, our philosophy of government, and our free market capitalist based economy has made America the greatest civilization the world has ever known. No civilization can match us when it comes to individual freedom, personal security, economic achievement, ingenuity, gritty resolve, generosity, and world leadership.

America can only remain America by fostering and maintaining our pioneering heritage. That heritage must be combined with maintaining our free market capitalist based economy and strong adherence to the principles and laws set forth in the Declaration of Independence and the Constitution. It is these four components that have provided the foundational structure for our extraordinary success.

Unfortunately, the good life these components have provided has spoiled our American society resulting in unrealistic expectations, gluttony, polymorphous perversity, other perversities, and movement toward fanciful utopian Marxist ideology. We have a lack of memory, understanding, and appreciation of how America became America and the many historical sacrifices made for our personal good. As I pointed out in chapter 4, we are just like the Israelites and headed toward self-destruction. Here is a great quote by Peter Marshal of *A Man Called Peter* fame who was a Presbyterian minister and Chaplain of the U.S. Senate during the late 1940s. He said, "May we think of freedom, not as the right to do as we please, but as the opportunity to do what is right."

Here are two other great quotes on the topic. President Harry S. Truman said, "America was built on courage, on imagination and an unbeatable determination to do the job at hand." Another U.S. president said, "This danger is invisible to some … the steady creep of government bureaucracy that drains the vitality and wealth of the people. The West became great not because of paper-work and regulations but because people were allowed to chase their dreams and pursue their destinies." Who said this? President Donald Trump said it during his July speech in Poland. Much to the progressives' chagrin, the quote is very presidential, insightful, and one to be remembered.

Our society now uses the word "progressive" to describe what we used to call liberal. I guess that sounds more acceptable than Marxist, which is what progressive actually means. The word should more accurately be regressive—not progressive. Classic liberalism as I defined it in chapter 2 is fast becoming extinct, especially within the Democratic Party, and is being replaced by Marxist ideology—progressivism. Chapters 4 and 11 discussed that progressives want to make America their utopian fantasyland to achieve their sinister goal of power and control. Progressives do not see themselves as equals in society but rather as intellectual elitists who are above society as they accomplish their objectives. The dictates and laws they impose do not apply to them. They only apply to classic liberal ideologues who naively follow them or succumb to them and the rest of us who believe in traditional American ideology and are forced to obey their devious and diabolical authoritative acts.

In chapter 5, I discussed Cass Sunstein (one of the most progressive elitist thinkers on the planet) who wrote in his 2008 co-authored book titled *The Nudge* that people need public and private organizations to help them make decisions because people make poor choices and look back in bafflement. He also promoted that animals might be thought of as humans and be given legal status to sue in order to stem animal abuse. In defense of progressivism, one might say that Sunstein is not a classic mainstream progressive but a person who is wacko. But remember, he was a White House Czar under Obama who influenced national policy and is now back teaching law at Harvard (to our young people, I might add). Also, remember his progressive wife Samantha Power was our ambassador to the U.N. under Obama after serving as one of his White House advisors. I can give you many such examples. In my opinion, wacko and progressive are synonymous.

In chapter 10, I discussed Karl Marx and Friedrich Engels who wrote in their 1848 book titled *The Communist Manifesto* that poverty and starvation were products of the evil that resulted from a capitalist society. The book proposed that the evolution of Marxist theory begins with socialism and progresses to communism. They wrote this evolution would begin when the proletariat (the working class) is fed up with their plight and orchestrate a social revolution against the bourgeoisie (the capitalist class that owns most of society's wealth and production). They said this revolution would result in a society based upon socialism (progressivism).

I also discussed in chapter 10 that Max Horkheimer founded the concept of Critical Theory in 1930 at Frankfurt University in order to implement Marxist ideology throughout the Western world. The basis of Critical Theory is to "criticize" existing society in the most destructive way possible to bring "liberating change" as opposed to merely presenting society a Marxist political alternative, which had been proven to be unsuccessful. The purpose of Critical Theory was to bring down Western culture and religion in order to replace free market capitalism with Marxist-based ideology.

Critical Theory concentrated on touting society's repression of women, gays, and blacks. Another theme touted by Horkheimer was environmentalism. Environmentalism became a primary push to counter what he called man's domination of nature. As I discussed in the original book, the Marxist movement of Critical Theory started in the 1930s and only the name has changed. Critical Theory is now called "political correctness".

Another key person at the Frankfort School was Herbert Marcuse. He introduced the sexual element, which is central to Critical Theory. Marcuse's writings promoted a society of "polymorphous perversity" in which a person can "do their own thing". He wrote extreme material regarding the need for sexual liberation. Horkheimer promoted the bourgeois culture as being excessively devoted to labor. He expressed his demand for human sensual happiness that he claimed the bourgeois inherently had treated with hostility.

We routinely see this today as progressives push laws and regulations that diminish personal responsibility and independence and promote leisure and entitlement. Our traditional American social norms are being aggressively attacked to develop a society of excessive permissiveness. A recent Gallup poll said Americans believe the moral values in the U.S. have slipped to a seven-year low. Eighty-one percent said our moral values were only fair or poor and 77% said they are getting worse.

Even Halloween is not exempt. A major haunted house attraction in my community advertised that no one under 18 would be admitted after 8:30 P.M. because of "graphic sexual content" and "explicit language". One of my favorite local newspaper columnists said, "It's almost Halloween and you know what that means. Kids in costumes, candy, and graphic sexual content . . . what is concerning is the societal movement toward sexualizing everything that can be sexualized."

As bad as the Halloween story is, I ran across a recent news story that is much worse. Teen Vogue, a sister magazine to Vogue and published by Condé Nast, contained an article titled "A Guide to Anal Sex". I first learned about this on theblaze website which had a story regarding an outraged parent who put a video on Facebook expressing her anger as she burned the magazine article by article in a bonfire. She referenced several other sexually oriented articles in the magazine and demanded the magazine be removed from supermarkets, libraries, and convenience stores. I discovered several news stories on the Internet that both condemned and supported the Teen Vogue article. I found that very troubling. Why didn't 100% condemn the article?

Theblaze reported over 11 million people viewed the Facebook video. I could not confirm that number but whoever saw the video should have made their views known to Condé Nast. How about threatening to cancel any subscriptions they have with the 25 magazines Condé Nast publishes?

Here is what I learned reading the news stories. The magazine's target audience ranges from 11 to 17-year-olds. The author of the article promoted anal sex and anal sex toys to "prepare for the experience". Britebart quoted the article's author as recommending the insertion of sex toys to "warm up" for "larger things". This is for 11 to 17-year-olds??? Totally shocking and unbelievable!!!

The Teen Vogue staff responded to criticism by saying the criticism was based upon "bigotry" and "homophobia". Sound familiar? This is standard progressive defense against conservative backlash in such matters. I also hear a little Alinsky in that progressive response.

Theblaze and other news articles showed the magazine's digital editorial editor in a photo on Twitter in which he was kissing another man while outwardly holding up his middle finger toward anyone who was looking the picture. The text said the following, "Inundated with hate mail saying we promote sodomy and want teens to get AIDS. It's funny because I went to Catholic high school and had o [sic] sex education. I also had a teacher tell me gay sex was a sin in God's eyes. The backlash to this article is rooted in homophobia. It's also laced in arcane delusion about what it means to be a young person today." The author of the Teen Vogue article was quoted as saying she would never discontinue her mission to help young people better understand their bodies and how they work. As I read this stuff, the word "wacko" again comes to mind.

According to Wikipedia, the magazine's single copy sales had suffered a 50% drop in the first six months of 2016 and a new editor replaced the founding editor. I might add that the new editor is only 26 years old—hardly an experienced and mature publishing executive.

Publishing articles such as this in an attempt to increase sales would be one thing but I think this situation goes much deeper.

Vogue editor Anna Wintour tutored the original editor of Teen Vogue and is now the artistic director for Condé Nast publishing. Wintour was a personal member and active recruiter for Hillary's Hillblazers. Hillblazer members contributed a minimum of $100,000 to Hillary's presidential campaign. Teen Vogue and perhaps Condé Nast publishing in general is saturated with progressive ideology and is an excellent example of the progressive elitism we talk about that knows what is better for us than we do ourselves. Did you know that Hillary is now a guest editor for Teen Vogue? No surprise there!

I quoted a comment by Melissa Harris-Perry on MSNBC in chapter 13. She said, "We have never invested as much in public education as we should have because we've always had a private notion of children. Your kid is yours and totally your responsibility. We haven't had a very collective notion of these are our children. So part of it is we have to break through our kind of private idea that kids belong to their parents, or kids belong to their families, and recognize that kids belong to whole communities."

The article in Teen Vogue is Marcuse's polymorphous perversity at its finest or, more appropriately, at its worst. If our society eventually succumbs to domination and rule by progressive ideology, the Halloween story and the Teen Vogue story will only represent the proverbial tip of the iceberg and we are increasingly getting closer every day.

For example, I saw the trailer of a new show that began in September on Netflix titled Big Mouth. Netflix advertises the show as an animated series about reaching puberty. In actuality, it is an extremely crude "potty mouth" show depicting continuous masturbation by young boys. Netflix said it was OK because their genitals were not graphically shown. There was also reference to young girls and menstruation. I found the trailer so disgusting, distasteful, and crude that I quickly stopped watching it. The show has a mature designation but it is easily accessible to anyone at any age.

Even mainstream television is getting into the act. In September, CNN debuted its three-part special titled "This is Sex with Lisa Ling".

The first show was titled "Sex 101" and featured a California high school class where students are instructed on sex including how to put condoms on models of male genitalia. Theblaze said the class promotes how to have sex in homosexual relationships and provides clinics for free contraception. The Teen Vogue article would be great course material for this class. Is there parental oversight of this high school class? Does the course material comply with the majority of parents' values, expectations, and parental rights? Of course not! Don't forget what progressive Melissa Harris-Perry said.

Here are some examples from chapter 10 regarding government overriding of parental rights. Poor children as young as 10 years old in Washington State were getting taxpayer funded IUDs for birth control without parental knowledge. Guidelines on teaching gender identity and sex education were sent to Washington state schools for children in kindergarten through 5th grade without notifying parents. Schools in and around Denver, Colorado were buying $125 Birth Control Planning Kits from Planned Parenthood for males and females and giving them to students without parents' permission. Some of the kit's contents were what I would call very interesting to say the least? And finally, we talked about Oregon's new law that would allow children as young as 15 years old to undergo radical treatment, including surgery, for gender dysphoria without parental knowledge or permission and be paid for by taxpayers.

Ontario, Canada just passed a law titled The Supporting Children, Youth, and Families Act of 2017. The act allows the government to intervene if parents of children with gender identity issues do not accept their child's "gender expression". Norway has a new law that allows the state to decide about gender assignment for children as young as 6 years old if both parents cannot agree on the child's gender.

Indiana passed a law last year banning sex-selective abortions. Planned Parenthood requested and received a permanent injunction by a federal district judge to stop the law's implementation. You can guess who appointed the federal judge. We will discuss Obama and the federal judge issue later. Planned Parenthood unsuccessfully attacked a similar law enacted in Arkansas earlier this year. Ten states have passed laws banning sex-selection and Congress tried once but was unsuccessful.

Historical data from throughout the world shows baby boys far exceed baby girls in gender selection. Historical data for God's gender selection indicates he is about 50/50 which is good for the human race. Available information for the U.S. is mixed depending upon the source. Some information indicates selection would be about equal while other information indicates boys are preferred.

So what's next—manufactured babies from a laboratory? Just like buying a new car, you will be able to pick the colors and the features you want. Don't laugh. We are technologically getting closer every day and the progressives are on board to make it happen. I discussed throughout the original book the progressives' dehumanization of American society and its negative effect on our society's future success.

It just doesn't stop and is increasingly getting worse. A Daily Signal article written by Scott Yenor reported in August that Minnesota has now joined Washington State in promoting transgender ideology in elementary schools against the wishes of parents and has made "gender identity" toolkits available to teachers so that 5-year-olds can learn to explore their identities.

Also in August, it was widely reported that a kindergarten teacher in a California public school allowed a five-year-old student to change his male clothes to female clothes in class to reintroduce himself as a girl. The teacher read two books to the class on transgenderism that were written for kids. It is not surprising that several students went home very upset and concerned they might become the opposite sex. Several parents were very troubled by the teacher's actions but received little concern from the school board or other parents.

The president of the American College of Pediatrics, Michelle Cretella, M.D., strongly agreed with the parents who were upset. She had written an article in The Daily Signal in July regarding the fallacy of such actions and the dangers involved for the children. She received significant pushback from many professionals in the medical community who support this transgender activity. I find this progressive based pushback to be surprising and very troubling having worked in the healthcare industry for 40 years. Things have certainly changed since my retirement, which was only 10 years ago.

Scott Yenor, who wrote the above article regarding transgender ideology in Minnesota schools, is a visiting fellow at the Heritage Foundation and Professor of Political Science at Boise State University. He said the following in a second August Daily Signal article:

> Radical feminists aspire to revolutionize society in three ways. First, they seek to eliminate the different ways boys and girls are socialized, so that they will come to have very similar characters and temperaments. Second, they seek to cultivate financial and emotional independence of women and children from the family. Third, they hope to erase sexual taboos, embracing new ways for individuals to achieve sexual satisfaction outside of monogamous, procreative marriage. ... The new field for the rolling revolution with the greatest possibilities is transgender rights especially as applied to children. ... These laws, and others like them, aim to make children independent of their parents and to bless their sexual exploration even at a young age. They undermine the foundation of educating children toward marriage and family life. Under both of these scenarios, the line between the family and state comes to be drawn and redrawn by the state. ... The family will find it harder to function when its integrity is compromised.

In another Daily Signal article written by Yenor, he commented this movement began in America when a book titled *The Second Sex* was published in the U.S. in 1953. The book was written by French feminine activist Simone de Beauvoir and originally published in France in 1949. Yenor said Beauvoir's book began by asking the following question, "What is a woman?" He then said, "Her answer sets the stage for subsequent feminist thought: 'One is not born, but rather becomes a woman.' Society makes or constructs a woman's identity, not nature or

God. ... Sex, one's biology and the closely linked psychological traits, should not shape one's identity according to these feminists. Sex or biology is not destiny, they say. Women must emancipate themselves from all limits presented by biology or society."

Yenor said it was "radical feminist" Judith Butler who first established the formal link between transgenderism and feminism. I watched Butler on YouTube. She is no doubt one of the ultimate progressive intellectual elitists I discussed in chapter 11. I found her comments regarding feminism to be very strange at best. She looked and sounded like a person who was sexually non-traditional and looking for answers to explain and justify her own sexual identity. She and Sunstein would have some weird but copacetic conversations.

I researched Butler on Wikipedia and learned the following. She has taught at Berkley since 1993. No surprise there but I did find one surprise. Butler is the Maxine Elliott Professor in the Department of Comparative Literature and the Program of Critical Theory. Having a formal program on Marxist Critical Theory at a major university surprised me and is very troubling even at a very liberal university like Berkley. I wonder how many other universities have formal programs connected to Critical Theory? I had not connected the transgender movement to the feminist movement before I read Yenor's article and I have now connected the transgender movement to Marxist Critical Theory. I am sure Marcuse is smiling about that one.

I learned after I wrote the above that Yenor has received extreme criticism from progressive activists and Boise State facility and students. There is an intense effort to get him fired. The university has refused to fire him but has not defended his right to free speech in expressing his opinion. Yenor said he now feels like an "alien" on campus. One of the Boise State professors said she believes in free expression but the opinion expressed by Yenor, "... violated clear policies that govern our institution, our statement of shared values, and the State Board of Education policy regarding academic freedom and most important, our concern for our students."

Which is it—free expression or not? The professor can't have it both ways. Actually, she can. She's a progressive. I discussed throughout the original book the extreme hypocrisy practiced by progressives. This is another example of progressives and their followers demanding tolerance and acceptance for their ideology while at the same time showing intolerance and anger toward those who do not follow that ideology.

The transgender movement in America is not a movement to prevent discrimination as it claims. It is part of the movement to destroy traditional American values by misleading society and brainwashing our children. I don't know about you but I find this "stuff" to be real creepy. I wonder how many average Americans know what I have just presented about the transgender movement and the resulting implications for our country? I can assure you the answer is very few at best!

Life is not one big social experiment to provide progressive elitists intellectual enjoyment and the more diabolical progressives a human palette to exercise power and control. Always remember that the basis of political correctness, which was originally called Critical Theory, is to criticize existing society in the most destructive way possible. Its purpose is to facilitate change and bring down Western culture and religion in order to replace free market capitalism with Marxist-based ideology. Political correctness makes society much easier to manipulate and control by creating a false and unstable environment. A society in internal conflict and experiencing instability is much easier to achieve dominance over and inflict change upon than a society that is content and in a stable state.

Although efforts have been going on for many decades by progressives to implement their Marxist ideology, it has only been during the eight years under the Obama administration that they have been able to seriously began morphing our society from one based on traditional American values to one that would make Horkheimer and Marcuse proud. To that end, the progressives are doing anything and everything in their power to stop President Trump and his administration from nullifying the progress they made during the Obama presidency. We are now going to focus on those progressive efforts and the immense danger that brings to the future of American society.

Let's start with the constant personal attacks on our president. One can think what they want about Donald Trump and the feelings are mixed, even among supporters. He certainly is a non-traditional presidential maverick. Actually, that is how he got elected; however, the impulsive behavior he has exhibited in his Tweets and personal comments have too often been inappropriate and gotten him in trouble unnecessarily. He becomes his own enemy and with all the political enemies he has, he doesn't need that—nor does the country.

In general, Trump's maverick behavior doesn't bother me but he needs to tone it down. Ed Rollins, one of my favorite conservative political pundits, said it well with regard to Trump's lack of discern in his messaging. He said, "Don't think out loud." I have observed some improvement since he became president. I do not know how much of the improvement is due to his maturing in his job as president, his new communications staff influencing his messaging, or a combination of both. I would bet on a combination of both.

The president also needed to seriously tone down his management style. The U.S. Government is not a business owned by a single individual who can run it in any manner they wish without backlash and legitimate criticism from others. Trump now works for American citizens, not himself. The way he managed his White House staff and his Cabinet in the beginning needed significant improvement. It appears that making John Kelly the White House Chief of Staff has been a great move in that direction. The manner in which he fired James Comey was atrocious no matter what Comey had done. His open criticism of Attorney General Jeff Sessions for not recusing himself on the Russia collusion matter and being a weak Attorney General was extremely inappropriate. The firing of Tom Price was an improvement but not perfect.

Sessions testified before Congress that he recused himself after looking at department rules and consulting with a Department of Justice (DOJ) ethics officer. When he responded to the news media regarding Trump's criticism, he came across as a very principled and honorable person. The Federal Bureau of Investigation (FBI) has more recently said that Sessions was not required to disclose any meetings with Russian officials as long as it was within his duties in Congress. This contradicts what Sessions said when he recused himself. Your guess is as good as mine on that one. During Sessions first months in office, I began to question his ability to get the DOJ back on the right track and clean up the corruption that began under the Obama administration. He finally appears to be doing so.

Matters between Trump and his staff should be discussed and resolved in a professional manner behind closed doors. Any dismissals should be professionally announced. The presidency is not a television reality show like The Apprentice. Surprisingly, after what I just said, he is reported to be a good listener and delegator.

Trump's leadership style and the philosophy I expounded in my book titled *Exploring Great Leadership* are at odds but I am seeing continuous improvement in the way Trump conducts himself as president. I wrote in the book that often one's strength is also one's weakness. The reverse of that statement can also be true. In that vein, Trump's maverick and sometimes bullheaded behavior coupled with his resolve to achieve his agenda is what this country needs to counter the harm that has been inflicted on us by the progressives during the Obama presidency.

It would be difficult, if not impossible, for a traditional politician to push sufficiently hard enough to get the job done and to endure the personal attacks produced by the current progressive political environment. For that reason, I fully support President Trump in his often unorthodox efforts to save America from progressive ruin. I also want to give him credit that he has become more presidential in the way he acts and what he says while at the same time maintaining his mental toughness and maverick behavior.

We see the enormous negativity and pushback Trump encounters and I greatly appreciate his tenacity to follow through with his campaign promises even in the face of unprecedented opposition by the progressives, the news media, and even some republicans. I find it utterly stunning and shameful that democratic and republican politicians who are not progressive and the liberal news media fight Trump in such a way that is so harmful to America. They are so focused upon their own interests they appear clueless to the damage they are doing to our country. Maybe they're not clueless and don't care. Who knows?

The news media and the progressives recently stooped to an all time low in their criticism of Trump. Representative Frederica Wilson (D., FL.) went on a tirade against Trump accusing him of being insensitive to a Gold Star widow when he called her to offer his condolences. Wilson also said that Trump could not remember the soldier's name when he called. Wilson was a friend of the family and heard the call on a speakerphone. Trump said he was respectful and did remember the soldier's name. The Gold Star widow did not respond to news media requests for comment.

I have no doubt that Congresswoman Wilson did this to stir up negativity toward Trump and gain notoriety for herself. She routinely dresses in attention-getting outfits including colorful cowboy hats to match each outfit. I heard her giddily say on television that she has become so important that the White House is following her and she will have to tell her kids that she is now a rock star.

After days of ranting by Congresswomen Wilson, the Gold Star widow did appear on George Stephanopoulos' CBS show and said Wilson was telling the truth. I have no doubt the soldier's widow was used for political purposes to make Trump look bad. I also saw a CNN host try to get another Gold Star family to attack Trump during an interview but they did not take the bait.

This isn't the first time Stephanopoulos went after Trump using a Gold Star family. He interviewed Trump before the presidential election and obtained statements from him that were used by the Gold Star Khan family to be very critical of Trump at the Democratic National Convention? I can still see Mr. Khan on the podium waving a copy of the Constitution as he ranted against then candidate Trump. I absolutely believe the incident at the convention was a setup against Trump by Stephanopoulos and the Democratic Party as was the recent interview with the Gold Star widow.

There was such a continuous firestorm by the news media and progressives criticizing Trump that John Kelly appeared at a daily White House press briefing and defended the president. Kelly talked about his conversation with Trump advising him how to make the calls to the Gold Star families and said he told Trump what was said to him when his son was killed in action. It was almost exactly what Trump told the

Gold Star widow. Kelly remarked at the press briefing, "I was absolutely stunned when I came to work yesterday morning and brokenhearted at what I saw a member of Congress doing. Absolutely stuns me. And I thought at least that was sacred." Kelly said he went for a walk at The Arlington National Cemetery afterword.

General Kelly called Wilson an "empty barrel" at the press briefing. Wilson, who is black, responded that Kelly was a racist. Calling someone a racist or some group a racist group is a common accusation used by progressives, both black and white, to put down those who are in opposition with them.

The news media and the progressives then went after General Kelly with almost the same gusto as they went after Trump. They were doing the same to Kelly, who is a Gold Star father, as they were accusing Trump of doing to the Gold Star family he called. Nothing is off limits to these people. It is totally disgusting. Where is the morality? More importantly, where is the pushback by Americans toward this behavior? It is examples like this that make me believe our American society is dangerously close to falling over the progressive cliff of no return.

Before we move on, I will share one more example of progressive and news media hypocrisy. I think Sarah Huckabee Sanders does an outstanding job as White House press secretary. Her job is made significantly more difficult than it normally would be because of the press negativity toward the Trump administration. She is only the third women and the youngest woman to ever hold that position. A twice Pulitzer Prize winning columnist for The Los Angeles Times wrote the following, "Sanders looks more like a slightly chunky soccer mom who organizes snacks for the kids games. Rather than the fake eyelashes and formal dresses she puts on for her news briefings, Sanders seems as if she'd be more comfortable in sweats and running shoes." He also called Sanders a liar, a failure, and a pro at being ignorant.

He said these things after commenting that Ivanka and Melania Trump are closer to the Barbie Dolls in short tight skirts that he envisions Trump preferring behind the press briefing podium. After receiving significant criticism, the columnist apologized to the Times readers and to Sanders for "a description that was insensitive and failed to meet the standards of the newspaper".

Here are the points I want to make. First, I cannot believe that his apology was sincere. He apologized only after he got in trouble. His malicious ranting, which he has done before, doesn't say much for the integrity of the Pulitzer Prize either. Secondly, this is classic progressive hypocrisy. Progressives constantly profess to be for women's rights. Sanders is a great example of a successful women and role model for young women to follow. How about his degradation of Trump's wife and daughter? There are many such examples of progressive hypocrisy throughout the original book and in this Epilogue.

Let's get back to the Trump presidency. There was an editorial in The Wall Street Journal by Holman Jenkins, Jr. who is a columnist, editorial writer, and member of the editorial board. The editorial contained the following comments, "Trump is many things but he is not an idiot … like many presidents, (he) now is struggling to apply his mostly irrelevant knowledge to a job he is poorly prepared for … his election was exactly what you want in a democracy, a timely message from the electorate to the class of people who make it their profession to try to lead us."

Cal Thomas wrote the following, "All the pieces are now in place to yank America back from the brink. This is an opportunity that comes along once in a century. Success will silence the critics, who won't go quietly and accept defeat. If Trump succeeds in all he has promised, he will have saved the country from disaster. It will be said of him that he really did make America great again."

I have often wondered, if a more laid-back conservative like Mike Pence was president, what degree of negativity and pushback he or she would receive? Would it be as aggressive as it is toward Trump? There is no way to know but I believe the degree of negative aggressive behavior by the progressives is dictated by the perceived magnitude of threat to their agenda.

The presidential election was in November 2016. Progressives across the country, with significant help from Obama administration resources, began their campaign to smear Trump as a non-legitimate president after he won the republican primary in June 2016. They also began to work toward his impeachment if he were to very unlikely be elected president. Several of the Hillary Clinton political operatives that I referred to earlier went to work for the Democratic National Committee (DNC) after Hillary's defeat and have continued their dastardly deeds to smear Trump's reputation and make him appear non-presidential. There are many progressive individuals, progressive organizations, and progressive politicians who are involved in this effort. I have no doubt there is a degree of collaboration among these different factions in their effort to destroy the Trump presidency.

Accusations regarding Trump's sexual aggressiveness toward women were leaked to the press before he became president and, unfortunately, it appears that some of them were true. One specific allegation involving sexual misconduct is very significant and all indications are that it is not true. I am sure you are aware of the intelligence dossier on Trump that was put together by an ex-MI6 British intelligence agent working for a private British intelligence organization hired by Fusion GPS, a Washington, D.C. based opposition research firm. The agent is not James Bond—he is Christopher Steele. Bond would never participate in such farcical rubbish. Steele's 35-page intelligence dossier accuses Trump of potentially being subject to blackmail by Russian agents because they have information on him regarding sexual trysts in Russia and inappropriate dealings with Russian banks.

The news media first mentioned this intelligence dossier in the fall of 2016. CNN and BuzzFeed reported details of the dossier in January 2017. The Washington Free Beacon had used Fusion GPS for opposition research on Trump until he became the republican presumptive nominee at which time they ceased doing so. It has recently been reported and confirmed that the Clinton Campaign and the DNC paid Fusion GPS over $10 million dollars that resulted in the so-called Trump dossier. There are unconfirmed reports that the FBI also funded the dossier and used it as a basis to spy on the Trump campaign. Isn't that interesting? The Media Research Center reported that our un-news media (as I labeled the news media in the original book) at CBS devoted a whopping 69 seconds to this new revelation; however, that is better than ABC and NBC which devoted 0 seconds each.

The dossier is extremely important but not because it focuses on alleged improper conduct by our president. The more that is discovered about the Trump dossier, the more it supports my conspiracy theory that the progressives including the DNC, the Hillary campaign, and the Obama administration including Obama himself colluded in spying on Trump during the presidential campaign. My theory is further supported by the recent demotion of a senior FBI official because it was discovered that he concealed he met with the co-founder of Fusion GPS during the presidential campaign and after Trump was elected. The FBI official's wife was employed by Fusion GPS to investigate Trump.

The dossier was given to both British and U.S. intelligence agencies including the FBI and has been referred to many times by U.S. government officials. It could also be the basis of the Russia collusion investigation by Robert Mueller. The Director of the FBI, leaders of our intelligence community, and Obama reportedly shared it with Trump himself in a January meeting before Trump took office. This all took place even though none of the information in the dossier has ever been substantiated.

There is evidence according to theblaze that Obama's campaign arm, OFA, might have contributed approximately $800 thousand to the project. That's another interesting tidbit! There are also unconfirmed reports that the Russian government was involved in its creation. Wow, what an interesting twist if true! Isn't this the kind of activity that progressives accused Trump and his campaign staff of participating in and is being investigated by Mueller?

Kimberly Strassel of The Wall Street Journal apparently agrees with me. She wrote in one of her editorials, "The Washington narrative is focused on special counsel Robert Mueller's probe. But the ferocious pushback and unseemly tactics from Democrats suggest they are growing worried. Maybe the real story is that Democrats worked with an opposition-research firm that has some alarming ties to Russia and potentially facilitated a disinformation campaign during a presidential election." Strassel went on to say that the news media has its own "conflict of interest" since they have been "colluding" with Fusion GPS for years. I read that Fusion GPS is where the news media obtains a significant amount of its "political smut". No surprise there.

The Senate Judiciary Committee wants to talk to Fusion GPS about the Trump dossier and other activities in which they might have been involved concerning Trump and his election team. Two company leaders were subpoenaed to appear before the committee. I heard they pleaded the Fifth Amendment on every question. I also heard the committee democrats are pushing hard to protect Fusion GPS leaders. I wonder why?

The Steele report was reportedly used by the Obama administration to obtain a Foreign Intelligence Surveillance Act (FISA) warrant from the FISA Court to spy on a person named Carter Page who had a connection to the Trump Campaign. At the time of this writing, the FBI has neither denied nor confirmed this took place. All indications are that it was used. The FISA Court was very critical of the Obama administration for not guarding the civil rights of U.S. citizens who were innocently spied upon during their surveillance efforts. Guarding citizens' rights in this situation is called minimization. Circa News reported very damning information accusing the Obama administration of using government intelligence agencies to spy on Americans who were political opponents. I heard Senator Rand Paul (R., KY.) say on television that he believes hundreds and hundreds of people have been spied on including himself and other members of Congress.

I have zero doubt this reported spying by the Obama administration includes Trump and his campaign team. Remember when Representative Devin Nunes (R., CA.), Chairman of the House Intelligence Committee, privately reviewed documents on this issue and publicly stated it was true? Ranking member Adam Schiff (D., CA.) heavily criticized Nunes for doing so and demanded he recuse himself from the committee's investigation. Kimberley Strassel wrote the following in a Wall Street Journal March editorial, "All this engineered drama served to deep-six the important information Americans need to know. Mr. Nunes has said he has seen proof that the Obama White House surveilled the incoming administration—on subjects that had nothing to do with Russia—and that it further unmasked transition officials. This is a crime. ... To sum up, Team Obama was spying broadly on the incoming administration."

The House Ethics Committee recently cleared Congressman Nunes of any wrongdoing. Interestingly, it has just been reported that during a recent Intelligence Committee hearing involving Trump's son, Schiff left the hearing several times. The hearing was confidential and behind closed-doors. There were leaks to the press as the seven hour hearing was in progress that were negative toward Trump, Jr. and untrue. It is believed that Schiff was the source of those leaks. This is classic Schiff behavior, which is very unethical just like his behavior toward Nunes.

The House Intelligence Committee issued subpoenas in late May to the FBI, Central Intelligence Agency (CIA), and National Security Agency (NSA) for documents pertaining to the unmasking of names in 2016. Unmasking is the public releasing of the names of U.S. citizens who were involved in minimization. The committee specifically requested information regarding the following members of the Obama administration: National Security Advisor Susan Rice; CIA Director John Brennan; and U.N. Ambassador Samantha Power. It has recently been reported that the committee is now looking at Ben Rhodes who was a very controversial Obama White House official.

I wonder if the committee knows something that we don't? Are we seeing a pattern? Could the Obama White House have spied on the opposition and used the process to falsely condemn Trump campaign associates like Gen. Michael Flynn? I believe they did and my belief becomes stronger and stronger as information is continuously uncovered.

I saw Susan Rice say during a television interview on PBS that she never requested any Americans to be unmasked and then, after it was exposed that she did, say during a MSNBC interview that she did so but what she did was absolutely legal. Which is it? She said in the second interview, "I leaked nothing to nobody ..." Maybe the double negative says it all. The House Intelligence Committee has interviewed Rice but it was behind closed-doors and nothing has been released about the meeting. She has suggested that race and gender are playing a part as to why she is under scrutiny. That's nothing but classic progressive BS.

The very liberal American Civil Liberties Union (ACLU) said the newly disclosed intelligence violations are some of the most serious to ever be documented and they questioned our intelligence agencies ability to police itself and safeguard the privacy of Americans as guaranteed by the Constitution's Fourth Amendment. It is extremely interesting that government policies were changed just before Obama left office that allowed a significantly greater number of government employees to have access to classified information.

In June, Senate Minority Leader Chuck Schumer (D., N.Y.), invoked a little used parliamentary rule to shut down a closed-door meeting between the Senate Judiciary Committee and government intelligence officials that was scheduled to examine the unmasking issue. The progressives are fighting as hard to cover up misdeeds by the Obama administration, as they are to convict Trump and his campaign staff of misdeeds they didn't do. If the truth is ever finally exposed, I have no doubt the Obama administration, not the Trump administration, will own the biggest government scandal in U.S. history—routinely using government resources against political opponents and others who are in opposition to their agenda and covering up those actions from the American people.

Two other potential scandals for democrats are beginning to be exposed. Representative Debbie Wasserman Schultz (D., FL.), who I discussed in chapters 2 and 10, is under scrutiny because of her relationship to a Pakistani family and one of their friends who were hired as House IT workers. They also worked for the DNC. Hmm? Could they have sold DNC information rather than it being hacked?

The Pakistanis were banned from working for dozens of House members when they came under investigation for "stealing equipment and committing serious violations". The serious violations have not been publicly defined. Some of those House members served on committees that handled sensitive classified information. It was reported that the Pakistanis were paid $4 million since 2009 and many of them did not even show up for work. All the Pakistanis except their leader fled back to Pakistan when the investigation began. The leader was arrested for bank fraud as he was fleeing the country at a later time. Schultz was still paying him.

I saw a video in which Schultz threatened the U.S. Capitol Police Chief if he did not immediately return her equipment that was being examined in the investigation. Schultz's actions toward the Capitol Police could be a crime in itself. I think what we currently know about this situation is only the tip of the iceberg of what was going on. Was it incompetence? Was it espionage? Was it blackmail of House members? Did it affect U.S. security? Will we ever find out? Currently, progressive politicians and the mainstream news media are ignoring it. There is no doubt this should be a major scandal for the Democratic Party.

As this book is going to press, I heard Glen Beck discussing this issue on his radio show. He said there is the potential of this Pakistani family being involved in a money-laundering scheme for the Hezbollah terrorist group through a used car dealership. Hezbollah is based in Lebanon but was founded by and funded by Iran. Politico had just reported that the Obama administration protected members of Hezbollah who were smuggling cocaine into the U.S. and money laundering the profits through used car operations—a $1 billion a year operation.

The Drug Enforcement Agency (DEA) had been working on shutting down this drug operation for eight years under Project Cassandra and was forced by the DOJ to delay and reject any prosecutions during the Iran Deal negotiations. After the Iran deal was completed the entire investigation was shut down. A DEA agent was quoted by Politico as saying, "Hezbollah operates like the Gambino family on steroids and Safieddine (the group's leader) is its John Gotti. Whatever Iran needs, Safieddine is in charge of getting it for them." Looks like Iran got Safieddine whatever he needs.

This appears to be another very serious government corruption scandal by the Obama administration. It was difficult to keep up with all the Obama administration scandals when I wrote about them in the original book and they just keep on coming. What else is out there we do not know about? It is no surprise that CNN, CBS, NBC, and ABC all ignored this story—a very sad commentary for the mainstream news media.

If what Glen Beck discussed morphed into reality, wouldn't that be interesting and what impact might that have on Schultz and the Democratic Party? Schultz may encounter other criminal problems. Donna Brazile, past DNC Chairwomen, said in her new book that the Clinton Campaign colluded with the DNC to rig the nomination process to ensure that Hillary defeated Bernie Sanders. She said the Clinton campaign paid off the DNC's debts and then took control of the DNC financial, strategy, and staffing decisions. Fox News' legal analyst and commentator, Gregg Jarrett, said what the Clinton campaign did is illegal. He commented, "The Clintons are escape artists that would make Houdini proud."

The Senate Judiciary Committee under Chairman Chuck Grassley (R., IA.) has launched a probe into the Hillary and Bill Clinton Russian uranium scandal that I discussed in chapter 9, which reportedly netted the Clintons $145 million dollars for their foundation and Bill $500 thousand for a speech in Russia. This investigation resulted from a report by The Hill stating the FBI had uncovered evidence during a four year investigation that Russian nuclear officials were involved in a racketeering scheme involving bribes, kickbacks, and money laundering with the goal of expanding Putin's atomic energy business on U.S. soil. The FBI did not bring charges against those involved until after the Russian uranium deal was approved by the Obama administration.

The investigation was supervised by then-U.S. Attorney Rod Rosenstein, who is now Deputy Attorney General in charge of the probe involving Russian meddling in the presidential election, and also by then-Assistant FBI Director Andrew McCabe who is now Deputy FBI director. Guess who was the FBI Director during this time? It was none other than Robert Mueller who is the special council investigating the alleged election interference by the Russians.

This recent revelation by The Hill raises several questions. Who in the Obama administration outside of the FBI was aware of the Russian uranium deal investigation and why didn't they raise red flags before the uranium deal was approved? If no one in the Obama administration was aware (which I seriously doubt), why didn't the FBI intervene? Were there bribes to government officials other than Hillary? Can the current Russia Trump campaign collusion investigation be unbiased, fair, and thorough? Many of the people in charge of this investigation were also in charge of the Russian uranium deal investigation. Could there be information regarding the Russian uranium deal investigation that would be embarrassing or incriminating if discovered during the Russia Trump campaign collusion investigation?

I find this revelation about the Russian uranium scandal to be stunning. Every effort needs to be made by The Senate Judiciary Committee to provide the public with a full accounting of what happened. Or, will this investigation be another one that quietly fades into the sunset with no accountability for those involved? The American public has a right to full disclosure of any government corruption and the assurance by Congress that it will not happen in the future. The mainstream media has totally ignored the story, which is reprehensible but not surprising.

As I write, revelations continue to unfold almost daily regarding those involved in Mueller's investigation of Russian collusion in our presidential election. As these revelations occur, I have greater and greater concern that the political corruption instilled in the DOJ by Eric Holder is still endemic in the department and it may be impossible to obtain an honest outcome. It also raises the question of what else is going on in the DOJ in support of the progressive movement.

I often wonder how patriotic well-meaning public servants in the FBI persevere in their apparent politically corrupt environment. The FBI has over 35,000 employees. I hope a number of these employees eventually speak out and tell the truth as did the FBI informant who worked for six years as an undercover agent on the Russian uranium deal and is being interviewed by Grassley's committee. His testimony and supporting documents have incriminating potential against the FBI and Hillary. Stay tuned on this one.

Information leaks that were negative to Trump and his administration have been unprecedented. Judicial Watch reported there were 125 national security leaks during Trump's first 126 days. That is seven times the average number incurred by Bush and Obama during their first six months in office. The leaks have now significantly diminished. Maybe that is because they finally arrested a government leaker. Most, if not all, of the leaks that were damaging to the president have been found to be total lies. I sometimes wonder if the government is so infiltrated with progressives that it will be impossible to stop leaks supporting progressive interests.

James Comey in his testimony before the Senate Intelligence

Committee said the leaks "largely reported" by the news media were "false in the main". He said his leak to The New York Times was accurate. That is another story in itself. Leaking his personal notes to the public (which are, in effect, government documents) would have serious legal repercussions for Comey, if the issue were to be pursued.

Comey may have a more serious issue hanging over his head. The Senate Judiciary Committee discovered Comey begin drafting the infamous statement he made on television exonerating Hillary Clinton approximately two months before the investigation was completed. We have also learned the senior FBI agent who was in charge of the Hillary private email investigation changed the wording on Comey's statement from "grossly negligent" (which is the exact wording in the law to determine guilt) to "extremely careless". You will read later some of the things this agent texted that were very negative toward Trump. You can't make this stuff up! I heard more than one attorney say that "intent" did not have to be proven to be guilty, only that the act occurred. Hillary also signed a document when she took office as Secretary of State that she understood all government emails had to be transmitted on government equipment in order to preserve them as government records and for security reasons.

During Comey's testimony before Congress, he misled them about his public statement regarding Hillary. That could be a felony if pursued. I believe Comey knew that the DOJ was not going to prosecute Hillary under any circumstances and he was attempting to cover for his department and himself. This is one more example of government corruption under Obama and his progressive administration.

I read another Wall Street Journal editorial by Kimberly Strassel in September that agrees. She said, "Mr. Comey's meddling has never seemed to stem from some hidden partisan impulse, but rather from an overweening self-righteousness. But power can be misused as much in the hands of the sanctimonious as the corrupt. And it's overdue for congressional investigators to get to the bottom of precisely how much power Mr. Comey was exercising."

After ten months, Trump continues to be problematically behind in replacing Obama's staff with his own. In May, only 79 of the 554 people needing Senate conformation were confirmed and there were thousands more yet to be hired who did not need confirmation. Although this number has improved, he still has a long way to go. As of October, the Senate has confirmed less than one-half of Trumps executive branch and judicial nominees. That is the lowest number confirmed during the last four presidents.

Trump's administration needs to get their people in place to limit activity by those in opposition who are severely undermining Trump's agenda and therefore undermining America. In the administration's defense, it is not all their fault. Congressional Democrats have stonewalled appointees who need congressional approval to an unprecedented degree. This is especially true for federal judges. And, I was surprised to learn that the Senate only works in session a total of two and one-half days per week. Unbelievable, isn't it? The Senate Republicans have recently vowed that confirmations will improve.

The Daily Signal reported in February that approximately 95% of the political contributions by federal employees went to Clinton. The story said almost 1,000 employees at the State Department signed a letter opposing Trump's original executive order regarding the temporary travel ban and refugee policy. Townhall editor, Justin Holcomb, reported in March that at least 180 federal employees signed up for a workshop concerning worker's rights and expressing civil disobedience. Dozens more have attended support groups discussing opposition to the Trump administration. Holcomb also reported the following:

> Less than two weeks into Trump's administration, federal workers are in regular consultation with recently departed Obama-era political appointees about what they can do to push back against the new president's initiatives. Some federal employees have set up social media accounts to anonymously leak word of changes that Trump appointees are trying to make.

Fox News reported in July that the U.S. Postal Service had given 97 employees time off without pay to campaign for Hillary and six democratic senatorial candidates during the November election. The National Association of Letter Carriers paid them money that was equivalent to their salary. This is a violation of the Hatch Act and illegal.

A Kimberley Strassel May editorial in The Wall Street Journal talked about a radical progressive employee at the Environmental Protection Agency (EPA) who has the title of Scientific Integrity Officer. She was hired in 2013 to "root out all meddlesome science deniers". The EPA officer has been busy since Trump became president. The Sierra Club made a request to her that Scott Pruitt, Trump's new EPA Administrator, be investigated because of his attitude regarding global warming. She also planned a "scientific integrity" event and invited 45 participants. All invitees but one were radical progressive organizations. Strassel said, "This is a government employee using taxpayer funds to gather political activists on government grounds to plot—let's not kid ourselves—ways to sabotage the Trump administration." Strassel concluded, "The sooner department heads recognize and take action against that deep state, the sooner this administration might began to drain the swamp."

How about the progressives in Congress like Senator Schumer, House Minority Leader Nancy Pelosi (D., CA.), and their loyal in-step progressive minded congressional flock? They spend their entire waking hours trying to destroy the Trump administration and the conservative agenda rather than doing their jobs representing the best interest of Americans. I don't know which one is worse—Schumer or Pelosi. Pelosi is bad enough in her rambling, off the wall, and untrue comments but Schumer makes statements that are so atrocious and false that I question his sanity as he questions Trump's. Both Schumer and Pelosi said many times that both the House and Senate republican healthcare bills were "mean" and that "hundreds of people would die" if either were implemented. I once saw Schumer crying or faking crying as he said this. Jeez!

At the time of this writing, Schumer and Pelosi's newest rant is the bill passed in Congress to provide tax relief to the middle class and corporate America and to simplify the tax code. They both continually and emphatically proclaim the bill will only benefit the rich and hurt the middle class. Totally not true and they know it. It is amazing how

Schumer, Pelosi, and their progressive cohorts forcefully push falsehoods like these to destroy the republicans when the facts prove them wrong. Another missed opportunity for republicans to expose progressive BS.

Here are some interesting facts from chapter 8. The top 1% of income earners pay 40% of all taxes, the top 20% pay 84%, and 45% pay no taxes. Thirty-four percent of those who do not pay taxes receive money from the IRS in the form of refundable tax credits, which is a form of income redistribution. The only plan the progressive democrats ever have to help the American people is to preach and support political correctness issues and falsely tear down any real plan to help Americans that is proposed by republicans.

I understand and appreciate reasonable political bias but I can't listen to Schumer's or Pelosi's political views because they are so angry sounding and far from reality. For example, I heard Schumer say the following at a press conference regarding the republican Senate healthcare bill, "... we (the democrats) are talking about average American working people while they (the republicans) are talking about multi-billionaires ... that is why they are in so much trouble ... the American people are listening to our arguments." What planet has he been on? Did he not know the democrats had lost four out of four of the previous special House elections when he said that? One of them was the most expensive democratic campaign in history for a House election?

Every time I hear Schumer, Pelosi, and other progressive politicians state their political differences with republicans, they constantly focus on the premise that republicans only want to support the wealthy and democrats are for the average working American? That is not a political platform with substance. I guess the wealthy are now out and republicans are only for multi-billionaires. According to Forbes, there are only 540 billionaires out of a total U.S. population of about 326 million people. The republican's better change their strategy quick. That's not a lot of votes. I will share with you another interesting fact from chapter 8. The concept of "the rich get richer and the poor get poorer" is a Marxist catchphrase that began in the 1800's and used to criticize free market capitalism

Progressive democrats are a tired broken record in how they have distinguished themselves from republicans? Progressive democrats' favorite political hype is: tax the wealthy to help the middle class and the poor; promote women's rights; end racial inequality; support LBGTQ rights; protect and support illegal immigrants and refugees; etc. I had not seen the letter Q included with LBGT until I wrote the above. I learned that Q means questioning. I am a strong supporter of gay rights but this is out of control. What is the next letter going to be?

Progressives wrap all of the potential voters referenced in the above paragraph in a cloak of victimhood and portray themselves as their savior. Ziggy defined victimhood with great clarity in a recent cartoon. He said, "Sigh ... it's just not FAIR ... a person studies hard and diligently ... works tirelessly, ambitiously, competitively ... struggles against overwhelming odds to make it to the top! Anyway ... people LIKE THAT make it tough for people like ME!"

In reality, what have progressive politicians ever done that truly helped the people they purport to protect? Progressives push Marxist ideology at the expense of the majority of Americans who believe in traditional American values. This creates friction between the American majority and the minority segments of American society the progressives claim they are trying to help. And, ironically, the ideology and laws progressives push for minority segments of our society are for the most part harmful to them. The following are examples.

We have already discussed some of the issues surrounding transgender people. I recently read a USA TODAY newspaper article, which argued both sides of the issue involving transgender people serving in the armed forces. The reporter taking the side against the policy quoted a survey that showed 40% of transgender individuals attempt suicide in their lifetime. That is almost nine times the normal suicide rate. The same survey said 39% of transgender people reported they had experienced serious psychological distress in the prior month versus only 5% of all respondents.

I support transgender rights but the progressives have pushed the issue of transgender rights much too far in order to gain LBGT support. Transgender individuals who are in need of psychological help and people who are uncertain of their sexual identity (especially children) suffer because of it. I recently read another Daily Caller article by Dr. Cretella in which she discussed the issues regarding children who are pushed into this transgender phenomenon and afterwards suffer greatly.

Progressives have provided significant welfare handouts and passed wage and labor laws that enslave people in poverty and reduce employment opportunity rather than only helping those who are truly in need. I do not know of one example where progressive policies and practices have improved quality of life for Americans. There is example after example; however, where progressive policies and practices have decreased the quality of life for those they claim to support.

The economic policies and laws driven by conservative politicians actually have helped people avoid poverty, get out of poverty, and increased the quality of life for all Americans. I presented convincing data supporting this premise in the original book. I recently read an interesting comment on this topic in an op-ed by Cal Thomas. He said the unemployment rate in Singapore is about 2% because the country has no welfare for able-bodied people.

We will discuss later how progressive rhetoric regarding racism in America creates racial tension rather than improve race relations. How can progressives take such a hard stand on supporting massive Muslim immigration and the uncontrolled influx of Muslim refugees considering the inherent significant conflict between Muslim culture and the rights of women and the LBGT population?

Who are the progressives increasingly depending on for political donations and support? They say the republicans are for the rich and they are for the middle class but it is the progressive democrats who are increasingly depending upon the wealthy Hollywood elite, wealthy Wall Street executives, and other wealthy people for monetary support. I wrote about the hypocrisy of the progressive movement and their dishonest political hype throughout the original book.

So, where I am I going with this narrative? The progressive democrats do not have a rational political platform that the majority of voters can relate to as being in their best interest. Most progressive rhetoric is ideological hyperbole that is conflicting and inaccurate. The only real and operable political platform progressives have is to destroy the competition by any means possible. I repeatedly said in the original book that the only way the republicans can lose to democrats is to hand it to them on a silver platter and republicans are sadly continuing to do so.

The progressive Democratic Party has become a party of hate, hypocrisy, and intolerance. A great example is the Antifa movement composed of anarchists who say they practice anti-fascism. Really? They orchestrate violent demonstrations and rioting to prevent free speech and they are anti-fascist? These progressives are paid demonstrators, troubled people acting out, confused people trying to find themselves, or all three. It is ironic they call themselves anti-fascist but protest against America—the most anti-fascist political system in the world. That distinction for America will be in deep trouble if the progressives and their fringe groups like Antifa complete their takeover of our country.

How about the Black Lives Matter movement? Black and white progressives use the Black Lives Matter fringe group to spew hatred at police and between races. The movement never promotes or supports any solutions to legitimate issues incurred by "black lives". If they care so much, why don't they attack real problems such as the horrendous problem of blacks killing blacks in cities like Chicago or the problem of black ghettos or the failure of our inner city educational systems? Progressives do not care about real solutions. They want to stoke tension—not omit tension. They champion Black Lives Matter to support their social justice narrative of racial inequality in America.

A Rasmussen poll taken in August said 72% of Americans eligible to vote believe politicians raise racial issues to get elected. Only 13% thought politicians who raised issues of race wanted to address real problems. Why do they get elected? Good question; however, the race issue is much bigger than political elections.

I discussed in chapter 10 there was not significant concern regarding racism in America before Obama became president and the progressives started pushing the racial narrative? Racial discrimination has continuously improved since the 1950s and 60s and was disappearing at an increasing rate. When Obama took office, racial discrimination was not in excess of any myriad of discriminatory behaviors by all

Americans including blacks and other minorities that occur as a result of human nature? I used myself as an example of being discriminated against as an Eastern Kentucky hillbilly.

Every human being on earth, including minorities, has his or her biases and has discriminated against others in their mind, outwardly, or both. It becomes a problem when these biases become hurtful to the person or group of persons on the receiving end of some action or actions verbally, physically, or by restriction of their Constitutional based rights.

Past Secretary of State, Condoleezza Rice, recently said, "That Constitution originally counted my ancestors as three-fifths of a man. In 1952, my father had trouble reregistering to vote in Birmingham, Alabama. And then, in 2005, I stood in the Ben Franklin Room ... I took an oath of office by that same Constitution, and it was administered by a Jewish woman Supreme Court Justice. That's the story of America." The progressives never acknowledge or celebrate our achievements as a society because it does not fit their narrative of a flawed country that needs to be changed to a Marxist utopia.

We hear over and over how racist white America is against all minorities but particularly against blacks. Do you find it as astonishing as I do that we hear how America is such a horrible racist country but we never hear fact-based specific examples of racism. We only hear police brutality and wacko accusations by individuals who determine almost everything to be racist no matter how ridiculous it might be? The reason is that those promoting the concept of racism in America have no specific examples or facts to support their accusations because there are none of any substance. Even police brutality is largely a made-up narrative. I am sure these race baiters can nitpick and find random examples here and there but racism is not endemic in America.

Race-baiters also conveniently ignore that there are very specific and strongly enforced laws regarding people who are in a protected class, which includes race, gender, age, physical state, and mental state. I talked in chapter 10 about my personal experience as the CEO of a company with 5,000 employees and I can assure you that laws against discrimination involving those protected classes are strictly enforced. And, do not forget the classic Civil Rights Act of 1964.

The only example these people routinely tout is police brutality and the facts show that claim is not true. The real question is, "What is their motive?" Let's begin answering that question by debunking the police brutality myth. We will then take a brief look at the black race in America and lastly expose the real reason they tout racism as a problem in America.

Here are some interesting statistics from chapter 10. Blacks of all ages are murdered six times the rate of whites in cities with large black populations. Democrats govern these cities and blacks hold significant political power. The cities have poorly performing and unsafe schools, poor quality city services, and declining populations. In 2009, the 75 largest U.S. counties had the following statistics: blacks were roughly 15% of the population but committed 57% of all murders, 45% of all assaults, and 62% of all robberies.

The Washington Post published a 2016 article by Heather Mac Donald that said approximately 28% of police shooting fatalities are black and 54 % are white. From 2005 to 2014, 40% of cop-killers were black. The article also said that in 2015 the police shot 36 unarmed black males and 31 unarmed white males. Unarmed did not mean the police were not threatened by other means such as knives or physical bodily harm.

These statistics do not support the narrative expounded by Black Lives Matter and the progressives and are only a sampling of such data. Using general population data alone, as progressives do, results in politically biased statements that are misleading and inaccurate. I said many times throughout the original book that progressives never want to be confused with the facts when the facts do not support their narrative.

I recently listened to a seemingly very intelligent black female attorney defend the racism narrative in an interview with Tucker Carlson on his Fox News show. It was very obvious that she had no interest in an honest, factual, and realistic discussion. Her only interest was to push racism in America and thrust aside any convincing or factual discussion otherwise. I have said that one of my favorite pundits is Jason Riley who is also black. He commented in a recent Wall Street Journal editorial that data shows the rate at which police kill blacks has fallen by 70% since the late 1960s. He summed the issue up very well when he said, "An increase in press coverage of police shootings isn't the same thing as an increase in police shootings."

Walter E. Williams, a black professor of economics at George Mason University, wrote a very telling article in a September Daily Signal. He said, "That the problems of today's black America are a legacy of slavery, racial discrimination, and poverty has achieved an axiomatic status, thought to be self-evident and beyond question ... But as with so much of what's claimed by leftists, there is little evidence to support it." He went on to say the number one problem in the black community is the effects stemming from a very weak family structure. The article stated only 22% of black children in 1960 were raised in single parent homes but 50 years later that number was 70%.

Williams said children from fatherless homes are more likely to drop out of school, die by suicide, have behavioral disorders, join gangs, comment crimes, and end up in prison. He commented that at one time all black families were poor but today roughly 30% of blacks are poor. He continued that only 8% of two-parent black families live in poverty and families where the husband and wife both work that number drops to less than 5%. In black families headed by a single female, the poverty rate climbs to 37%.

Williams' article also discussed the negative impact that labor laws supported by liberals, labor unions, and even black politicians have had on black employment since the mid-fifties. Williams concluded, "The undeniable truth is that neither slavery nor Jim Crow nor the harshest racism has decimated the black family more than the welfare state has. ... The most damage done to black Americans is inflicted by those politicians, civil rights leaders, and academics who assert that every problem confronting blacks is a result of a legacy of slavery and discrimination. That's a vision that guaranties perpetuity for the problems."

Progressives only want to influence the black population to maintain the vast majority of black votes. When have you ever observed any progressive honestly do or say anything to improve race relations or help the black race improve economically? You haven't. You have only observed rhetoric and actions that create racial friction and promote a black welfare state.

A New York Times/CBS poll during Obama's first year in office showed 66% of Americans believed race relations were generally good. A Rasmussen poll taken during Obama's last year in office said 60% of likely voters believed race relations became worse during his presidency. As you well know, they have continuously gotten worse after he left office. How did we get where we are today? We can thank Saul Alinsky and his *Rules for Radicals*. I mentioned earlier that my wife and I watched a documentary on his organizing principles. The documentary included Alinsky's successful efforts to unionize Eastman Kodak in the 1960s, which serves as a primer for what the progressives are doing today regarding race relations.

Obama is a master organizer using Alinsky's principles and he is not alone. There are many other progressives involved in the shadow government who are also masters of the Alinsky tactics I discussed in chapter 4. Obama and his shadow government cohorts picked racism as the issue to organize and unite their ideological community and create conflict toward Americans who do not share their progressive ideology. They picked the police as the antagonist and police brutality as the symbol to ridicule and protest against. The enemy is anyone who does not ideologically agree with them.

The big question is, "What is the ultimate goal?" The goal is to use anger to divide America between ideological divisions. As I consistently assert, a divided America is a weak America and much easier to manipulate in accomplishing the progressive's dastardly deeds of power and control. How that power and control is obtained and any collateral damage incurred are unimportant side issues. This progressive action to split America apart is an enormous affront and threat to Americans of all races. It is extremely concerning that it appears a large number, if not the majority of Americans, are clueless about what is actually happening and are being sucked into the progressive web of deceit and manipulation.

The Democratic Party has not done as well as the Republican Party with white women in recent elections and, as a result, just recently added the "well-being" of women to racism for future election fodder against republicans. Conservative political pundits surmise the reason for the current Democratic Party onslaught against their own sitting congressional members such as John Conyers and Al Franken for inappropriate sexual behavior is preparation for the 2018 midterm and the 2020 presidential elections.

These pundits believe the democrats will proclaim they are the party that protects and supports the well-being of women and will use republicans like Alabama's Roy Moore and President Trump as examples of how the Republican Party does not. At the time of this writing, the progressives are already beginning to attack Trump for inappropriate sexual behavior toward women as they did during the presidential election and are suggesting Congress investigate him. This is another example of progressive hypocrisy. They claim they are for the "well-being of women" when in reality they are "using women" for political purposes.

A very progressive independent film company released a documentary in November that focuses on women who Trump allegedly sexually mistreated. These are the same women that accused Trump during his presidential run. After the film was released, the women held a press conference sponsored by the film company and appeared on national television talk and news shows. The film company is funded by several far-left organizations including Media Matters and George Soros' Open Society. No surprise there.

The progressives were successful in defeating Roy Moore in the Alabama Senate race by accusing him of inappropriate sexual behavior toward teenage girls in the late 1970s. I read several reports of what supposedly took place and although what he allegedly did was inappropriate, it was nowhere near the extent of the democrats' allegations. Many republicans in Congress believe Moore's loss was a blessing because he would have been an albatross around the Republican

Party's neck for the democrats to use as election fodder. I believe this progressive activity is the tip of the iceberg for the upcoming midterm elections and the next presidential election.

I guess the Russian collusion narrative isn't providing the results progressives were hoping for. If these progressive democrats spent half as much time seriously working to do good for the country as they do trying to destroy their competition, think of what Washington could accomplish.

Many of the people involved in the Black Lives Matter organization were also involved in the Occupy Wall Street movement. What does black lives have to do with Wall Street? That is a very good question that makes a very important point. I said earlier that these people are paid demonstrators, troubled people acting out, confused people trying to find themselves, or all three. It doesn't always matter what the organization is or the organizing issue might be as long as the participant feels it fits their personal needs.

A psychological research group named The Frontier Lab performed an in-depth study of Black Lives Matter through one-on-one interviews with its members and their study supports my analysis of these radical groups and their members. The study said the movement is rooted in Marxism and is based upon the "privileged vs. the oppressed" instead of the old school Marxist terminology of "haves vs. have-nots". The goal is to explain what is wrong with America, which is critical in taking down our democratic form of government. Those involved want radical social change through revolution and to take down the entire American system. They are against dissent and freedom of speech and chose to accomplish their mission through force, intimidation, and fear. I might add that this analysis applies to all progressives and progressive organizations—not just Black Lives Matter.

The Frontier Lab said Black Lives Matter is composed of professional organizers and followers. They divided the members of the movement into three groups: activists who seek empowerment, hope, community, and excitement; allies who feel guilt, seek community, want to alleviate fear, and are actively pursuing good; and operatives who feel pride, confidence, excitement, and purpose.

I found a quote on The Frontier Lab's website from a speech at a Black Lives Matter rally that was given by a professor at Cornell University. The professor appears to be a champion of Malcolm X and said, "We've got to build a grassroots, antiracist [*sic*] movement to defeat capitalism altogether and it's not going to happen at the ballot box. There can be no human system under capitalism. Capitalism is an anti-human system." I think his quote sums up well what America is up against with the progressive movement. The movement is continually getting stronger and more emboldened as social justice is used as a screen to hide their real motive of destroying traditional America and imposing a Marxist-based government.

Although the vast majority of Americans might think Antifa and Black Lives Matter are extreme examples of progressive behavior, they are not. One only has to look at all the anti-American demonstrations that began during the Obama presidency. Obama encouraged these demonstrations, as did other influential progressive politicians like Attorney General Eric Holder and New York Mayor Bill de Blasio. Oh, and don't forget Al Sharpton and his organization's involvement in orchestrating the violent racial demonstrations that I discussed in chapter 10 such as those in Ferguson, Missouri and Baltimore.

Demonstrations regarding racism have gotten more frequent since Obama left office. White nationalism and the topic of slavery have been added to police brutality as symbols to ridicule and protest against. The antagonists have been expanded to include anyone or any symbol progressives associate with these topics. I have no doubt that Obama is quietly involved. Do you ever wonder how the organizations that are involved in these demonstrations are funded? We will discuss that later.

In their aggressive efforts to coerce conservatives into submission, radical progressive groups routinely physically attack conservatives who are demonstrating peacefully to defend our American values. The worst example during Trump's presidency thus far happened in Charlottesville, Virginia. Protesters were peacefully protesting the proposed removal of a statue of Robert E. Lee. The news media, progressives, and even conservatives characterized these protesters as white nationalists, white supremacists, the Ku Klux Klan, the alt-right, neo-Nazi, and whatever they could think of to label the protest as totally racist in nature. Antifa and Black Lives Matter were counter-protesters but never mentioned.

Defending the honor of one of our country's most historical figures, who was "opposed to slavery" I might add, is not a racist protest. Lee wrote a letter to his wife in 1856 before the Civil War that said slavery was a "moral and political evil". Are George Washington and Thomas Jefferson next? They owned slaves.

Actually, Washington is. I read in The Daily Signal that the Christ Church in Alexandra, Virginia is going to remove plaques from their altars honoring both Lee and Washington because they are too divisive and might discourage parishioners from attending church. The church leadership said, "The plaques in our sanctuary make some in our presence feel unsafe or unwelcome." Really? I wonder what they preach in that church—certainly not tolerance, understanding, and forgiveness.

Washington was a founding member of the church in 1773 and attended for two decades. An August Rasmussen poll said 88% of likely voters opposed removing the names of Washington and Jefferson in public places or taking down statues in their honor.

I quoted Charles Barkley in chapter 10 and here is another one of his quotes to think about. He said, "I'm not going to waste my time screaming at a neo-Nazi who's gonna hate me no matter what. I'm 55years old. I've never thought about those statues a day in my life. I think if you ask most black people, to be honest, they ain't thought a day in their lives about those stupid statues."

In actuality, the Civil War was not even about slavery. In Chapter 10, I talked about the Civil War being primarily about states rights. President Lincoln had said during his campaign for president he would not abolish slavery if he was elected. The Southern States started the Civil War because the northern states were promoting federal legislation that was economically threatening to them. Slavery was a side issue.

Oh, by the way, the Cherokee Indians had both Indian slaves and black slaves, which they took with them on the Trail of Tears. Are progressives going to destroy monuments that recognize the Trail of

Tears? Absolutely not! It doesn't fit their narrative of a morally corrupt America.

In the past, the progressives have gone after Christopher Columbus because they blamed him for discovering the land that is now the United States and causing it to be brutally and wrongly taken away from the indigenous Indian people who lived here. Chapter 4 debunks that falsehood. He never set foot on what is now the United States. I doubt the progressives ever took time to study Native American history and culture to learn that the Indians viciously and cruelly began fighting each other long before the early settlers arrived. They fought each other because of historical tribal conflict and for land. In many cases the French, British, and U.S. military fought side by side with the warring Indian tribes. The French and early U.S. settlers also participated in significant trading with American Indians.

The U.S. government "purchased" significant areas of land from France, Spain, Britain, and Mexico that is traditionally labeled by progressives as land the U.S. "took" from Native Americans and Mexicans. Like I continually say, never confuse these progressives with facts and reality if it doesn't fit their social justice narrative. Always remember that progressives will say or do anything to present America as a flawed country to justify their push for a Marxist America. The information on Native American history is covered in chapters 4, 5, and 10.

The progressives now single out Columbus as being very cruel to the indigenous people he encountered on his voyages to the West Indies, which he actually did discover and occupy. One only has to study world history to learn that Columbus was one of many explorers on the sea and on land that reflected the culture of early civilizations. What Columbus did was commonplace around the world. Can you imagine the progressives criticizing Muhammad for his cruelty in enslaving the men, women, and children he conquered during his crusade for Islam? There are some claims that the men were killed and the women and children were put into slavery and also raped.

Another interesting fact is that one of the two Indian cultures that Columbus encountered in the West Indies were cannibals and fiercely attacked the other Indian culture when the opportunity presented itself. Both cultures had migrated from the South American continent. The world was a different place in 1492. In world history, the concept of indigenous people is very fluid. Civilizations were exploring all across the planet and it is sometimes hard to know who was there first.

Life on Earth has been messy since the beginning of humankind and will continue to be until the end of time. There never has been nor ever will be the ideological utopia the progressives portray to offer under their leadership. Actually, history has shown that humans are routinely suppressed and suffer under progressive Marxist rule. I discussed this extensively in the original book as well as this Epilogue.

Until recently, I doubted there was any geographic area on the planet where exploration and colonization didn't take place. My wife and I just returned from the Amazon River in Brazil, one of the most remote areas on earth, and learned there are still indigenous Indian tribes that have been isolated from exploration and colonization.

The Portuguese colonized Brazil in the early 1500s and it became an independent country in 1822. We personally observed how the indigenous Indians, Portuguese colonists, and African slaves have blended together as one nation over past centuries. Other nationalities have settled in Brazil in more modern times. We also learned that an estimated 40,000 indigenous Indians still live in the lower Amazon Basin and Brazilian law has prohibited human contact with them since 1986 in order to preserve the tribes' natural heritage.

Even though these indigenous Indian tribes are in actuality under the control of the Brazilian government, our guide said it is believed that most of these tribes have never had any contact with the outside world. The area is very large in landmass and the rainforest where they live is very dense. This isolation is extremely unusual, if not uniquely the only place on the planet.

Let's get back to Charlottesville. I vehemently oppose racism; however, as much as it bothers me to say it, people who support white supremacy have a right to peaceful protest just like any other American citizen. Actually, the ACLU defended the Charlottesville protesters' right to free speech until significant backlash caused them to rescinded their position. They used the excuse that their policy prevents them from supporting free speech if guns were involved. I thought the goal of the ACLU was to protect the free speech rights of "all" Americans as spelled out in the First Amendment of the Constitution.

The news media is so focused on the issue of racism in America that it was impossible to get accurate news regarding what actually happened that led to the violent confrontation but here is what I pieced together from news reports and the news footage I saw. The group that organized the protest and the other groups that were initially involved were white nationalist based groups and this was not their first peaceful protest in Charlottesville. The protest in question started as a peaceful protest against the removal of Lee's statue, not as a racial protest, and the protesters had a permit to do so. I heard an on-site reporter say it was the Antifa group that started the violence when they and the Black Lives Matter group showed up to counter protest. No surprise there.

It has been reported but not substantiated that Los Angeles based Crowds on Demand was hired by unknown progressives to recruit people to go to Charlottesville and create chaos. I saw a copy of the ad that Crowds on Demand put on Craig's List in the Charlotte, N.C. area. The ad was recruiting people at $25 per hour plus expenses to function as "enthusiastic actors and photographers" at their events, which included "everything from rallies to protests". Charlotte is a large metropolitan area that is 4½ hours from Charlottesville. This has Alinsky written all over it.

The Crowds on Demand website is rather innocuous but it says their president worked as a political organizer for Jerry Brown in his 2010 campaign for Governor of California. As you know, Jerry Brown is very progressive. That tells you something. I wonder what crowds the company might have provided for progressives in the past—maybe violent and nonviolent crowds against Trump supporters at Trump rallies?

I have no doubt the progressive underground is organizing and funding the vast majority, if not all, of the current violent and nonviolent protests that are anti-racist, anti-American, and anti-free speech. Their goal is to destroy American history and traditional American values and substitute history and values that support Marxist philosophy. It is a form of brainwashing our society, especially our young people, in order to accomplish their mission.

Charlottesville and other progressive city officials have told their police officers to stand down if violence occurs during peaceful demonstrations. These peaceful demonstrations are always in defense of traditional American values. I find it more than coincidental that Antifa always shows up at these demonstrations and commits violence toward the peaceful protesters as the police stand by and watch. I heard a peaceful protest organizer for religious values tell Tucker Carlson that the police stood by as Antifa attacked them. The police told this organizer they joined the police force to protect people but were told by their superiors not to intervene if violence occurs. I have no doubt that Antifa is the unofficial proverbial "goon squad" for the progressive left.

Much was made of "racial hatred" regarding the individual who rammed his car into a crowd of people leaving the violence in Charlottesville and unfortunately killed a young woman and injured many others. He was reported by the news media to be a neo-Nazi and associated with the original protesters. Everything I could find about him indicated he is a neo-Nazi but not associated with any of the protest groups. He was a lone wolf who in all likelihood has mental issues. Referring to him as member of one of the protest groups as the progressives and the news media did was inaccurate. Wolf Blitzer and another person at CNN even questioned that this individual's actions might have been the impetus for the terrorist attack in Barcelona. This is unbelievably incompetent reporting but not surprising for CNN.

I read an AP news article that said the progressive Charlottesville mayor had declared his city as the "capital of resistance" to President Trump and a movement began by the city to remove its Confederate monuments including Lee's statue. The mayor was quoted as saying, "We are a progressive tolerant city." The city doesn't look very tolerant to me. He also said, "About a year and a half ago Charlottesville decided to launch on the difficult but essential work of finally telling the truth about race. That made us a target for tons of people who don't want to change the narrative." The article said Charlottesville was "essentially a progressive island in a conservative part of the state".

The mayor and city government were reckless in setting up Charlottesville for pushback from those who oppose their progressive intolerance. As I said, I strongly oppose white nationalism but those protesters had a right to peacefully protest the city's actions that were against their beliefs. Ironically, but not surprisingly, it was the progressives themselves who started the violence but the peaceful white nationalist protesters got the blame.

I find the following very disturbing. I watched President Trump condemn the violence by "all" involved. He did so in very strong terms but did not specifically condemn the white nationalist groups by name who were defending Lee's statue and opposing progressive ideology. He received strong criticism from the news media including Fox News, progressives, democrat politicians, republican politicians, and even many conservatives whose opinion I respect. These people wanted Trump to condemn the original peaceful demonstrators as violent white racists and not condemn all protesters for their violence as he did. Had he done that, he would have in effect supported and encouraged radical violence by anti-American progressive fringe groups like Antifa and Black Lives Matter who reportedly started the violence in the first place.

Trump handled it masterfully by strongly denouncing the violence in its totality and not characterizing the situation as a violent racist hate event organized by white nationalist groups, which it wasn't. This is a great example of why Trump won the presidential election. He was elected to stop the progressive onslaught on our country and get back to true American values. Unfortunately, he was forced by public outcry to have a second news conference and condemn the violence by specifically naming some of the more well-known radical white supremacy groups who participated.

He did so to calm down the negative rhetoric but again also referenced all violent groups, which was not well accepted by his critics. He did not specifically mention Black Lives Matter or Antifa. I am sure any reference to Black Lives Matter would have created an unimaginable firestorm even though they are anti-America and anti-white radicals who promote the killing of police and started the violence.

During a later news conference regarding the rebuilding of the country's infrastructure, instead of asking Trump questions about his plans, the press repeatedly questioned him on his position pertaining to the violence in Charlottesville. I was extremely proud of Trump when he, out of frustration, strongly characterized the event as it truly was. He said the protest groups on both sides were at fault but the protest groups on the left began the violence by attacking the white nationalists groups. Trump also said this discord and hostility needs to stop for the sake of America. I was totally impressed that he called it the way it was and did not capitulate to progressive pressure to get on the racist bandwagon like Obama. Unfortunately, but not surprisingly, the backlash against Trump only became worse.

Based upon the facts of the matter, the continual comments criticizing Trump were very irrational and very inaccurate. They were accurately critical of radical white nationalist groups that support racism in America but gave a total pass to an extremely radical progressive anarchist group and an extremely radical progressive anti-police and anti-white group that caused the violence in the first place and have demonstrated again and again hatred for America.

Let's take a quick look at the number of radical groups on both sides of this issue. The only source I could find for comprehensive data was the far-left Southern Poverty Law Center (SPLC) that is the source used by most, if not all, news media. They reported the following number of white racially focused hate groups: neo-Nazis, 100; white nationalists, 99; and other, 78. The SPLC said all of these groups were in decline. Neo-confederates were listed as having 43 groups and were increasing in number.

Wikipedia estimates there are 24 Ku Klux Klan organizations with a total of 5,000 to 8,000 members. Remember the population of the U.S. is about 326 million. Considering what we hear, you would think the Ku Klux Klan is a major violent political force in the U.S. I am sure they love the attention they are getting. Otherwise, they would be totally irrelevant.

How about black racially focused hate groups? The SPLC reported 193 groups and increasing in number. What? We never hear about these groups creating racial unrest against white Americans. Why? It does not fit the progressive narrative. I also learned that white racially focused hate groups are common around the world. That doesn't fit the progressive narrative of a disgraceful racist America either.

In all my travels around the world, I have never found that perfect society and slavery is still common in many parts of the globe. Where is that Marxist utopia progressives want us to become? It doesn't exist and there is overwhelming evidence provided throughout the original book that the more a country adheres to Marxist ideology the more its citizens' opportunities and freedoms are suppressed in all aspects of their personal lives.

Trump's comments were again inappropriately related to race when he said during a speech that the owners of NFL teams should fire any "son of a bitch" who takes a knee during the National Anthem. The progressives made it a racial issue and to my great surprise many conservatives jumped on the bandwagon. Trump said his comment had absolutely nothing to do with race. It was about disrespect to our flag and to our country. He was 100% correct. Because of the controversy, there was some concern the progressives might use this discord as an opportunity to push getting rid of the American flag and the national anthem at sporting events; which would support their efforts in eroding national pride.

Professional football player Colin Kaepernick started the issue last year by repeatedly taking a knee during the Star-Spangled Banner before games. Townhall reported a Rueters poll that showed 72% of Americans thought his behavior was unpatriotic but only 61% said they did not support his decision to take a knee during the national anthem. What is that 11% thinking? I agree that Kaepernick has a right to protest but that is not the place or the way to do it. I might also mention that Kaepernick wore socks at the games that had pigs on them wearing police hats.

Did you know that the NFL said no last year when the Dallas Cowboys wanted to wear police decals to honor the five Dallas police officers killed by a black gunman who had hatred toward the police. The NFL also refused to allow a group of players to wear specially designed cleats on 9/11 in remembrance of those who died from the attacks on the World Trade Center. The players wore them anyway and were not fined only after significant public outrage. What hypocrisy by the NFL!

While the NFL teams were taking knees on a Sunday, a black radical shot and killed a 39-year-old white woman who has two young children and wounded six other people at a church in Tennessee. The NFL story was on the front page of The New York Times. The mass shooting was on page fourteen. We know what The New York Times would have done if the shooter was white and the victim was black.

The significant backlash against Trump by such a diverse group that crosses the political divide is part of an extremely disturbing trend. It glaringly reflects the damage that has been inflicted upon the American psychic by progressives regarding race relations. The overwhelming irrational critical reactions to Trump's comments indicate to me that our American society is becoming much more entrenched down the progressive road than I realized when I wrote the original book.

Americans who believe in traditional American values are not defending those values in a sufficient way to preserve them and their opposition is progressively becoming less. Pun intended! I am always amazed how easy and effective it is to overcome opposition, even strong opposition, if those seeking to accomplish change practice persistence and patience. It is a successful form of society brain washing. I wrote about this phenomenon regarding societal behavior in chapters 4 and 5.

In chapter 12, I shared the story regarding the overwhelmingly patriotic Tea Party rallies in Naples where thousands of men, women, and children lined a busy street and peacefully protested Obama's progressive actions during his first months in office. These rallies occurred on three separate occasions. My wife and I attended all three and the patriotism at each of these rallies was palpable. In chapter 13, I shared the story of Glen Beck's Restoring Honor rally on the Lincoln Mall, which had hundreds of thousands of patriotic Americans in attendance. There were many other patriotic rallies around the country as well.

There was so much enthusiasm and pushback to defend our traditional American values by the thousands upon thousands who attended these rallies. Where is the overwhelming enthusiasm to defend our way of life now? The libertarian based Cato Institute recently released their 2017 Free Speech and Tolerance Survey. The survey showed that 58% of Americans believe the current political climate prevents them from sharing their own political beliefs. Seventy-one percent of Americans believe the current politically correct culture has "silenced important discussions society needs to have". As I write about what is happening in America today, I question more critically than ever any optimism I have toward America staying America.

There was an expression of patriotic enthusiasm by a number of Americans, including my wife and me, regarding the anti-American actions by the NFL. Unfortunately, the level of enthusiasm was nothing like the rallies in Naples, Washington, and other parts of the country eight years ago. I am extremely disappointed at the lack of intense backlash by American society against the NFL organization and its players, coaches, and owners to put this anti-American outrage back in its hole. Even moderate pushback worked to a degree. Advertisers felt threatened, fans turned on the teams, and television ratings dropped. This caused the NFL organization and the teams owners to take a look at what was happening.

The NFL team owners met to discuss implementing a rule that all players have to stand during the national anthem but they disappointingly punted. The NFL commissioner held a news conference and stated the players "should" stand for the National Anthem but the owners failed to pass a rule. What a copout! If the pushback had been great enough, I guarantee you there would be no players taking a knee. It is situations like this that gives me the feeling that our country is slipping into the progressive abyss to never return. Where is traditional American enthusiasm? It becomes less every day.

My hat is off to our president for saying any NFL SOB that disrespected our country and our flag should be fired. He stood up to all the significant criticism he received by many people in and out of sports.

Before we move on, I want to share one more incident regarding racism and progressive propaganda I find disturbing. Out First Lady, Melania Trump, sent a collection of books to one high performing school in each state for National Read A Book Day. The collection included ten Dr. Seuss books. An elementary school librarian in Cambridge, Massachusetts rejected the books saying Dr. Seuss books were "steeped in racist propaganda, caricatures, and harmful stereotypes" and enforced "systematic racism and oppression". Dr. Seuss a racist??? Even Barrack Obama publicly professed to be a Dr. Seuss fan in 2015 and Michelle Obama read Dr. Seuss books to children on many occasions.

The librarian was also very critical of Betsy DeVos. She said books (I assume no Dr. Seuss books allowed.) should be gifted to schools where DeVos is punishing schools with closures and slashing budgets in underfunded and underprivileged communities where schools are marginalized and maligned. She needs to read chapter 9 and learn how the progressive governments in Chicago and Detroit throw significant taxpayer dollars at poor performing schools and only the number of teachers in teachers' unions and the union members' retirement benefits improve. Unfortunately, this librarian is another example of "push progressive ideology at all costs" and "don't confuse me with the facts".

Here is the part that bothers me most. The Cambridge school system released a halfhearted and lame response regarding the librarian's actions that in effect ignored what the librarian did. The librarian said she would suggest ten books for Melania and Donald Trump to read. A photo appeared on the school's Twitter account showing the books the librarian suggested and I would characterize them as progressive propaganda primers for young people.

There was a handmade sign in the photo that said, "Take a stand by taking a knee, sitting down, speaking up, and marching forward." The sign also contained a picture of three football players taking a knee. This is consistent with the progressive propaganda I discussed in chapter 10 that is being taught to brainwash our children to support and practice progressive ideology. In chapter 7, it was learned that the word "forward" in political statements like the one in the handmade sign has its roots in Marxism and is commonly used by communists and communist organizations.

We have just reviewed examples of what makes Horkheimer and Marcuse smile big in their graves. The greatest society in the history of the world irrationally and very critically beating itself up as progressives change American history and American traditional life from reality to falsehoods that support their hateful narrative of America to corroborate their Marxist agenda. It is Critical Theory at its best or, more appropriately, at its worst!

Here is an analysis I read in theblaze by Rush Limbaugh that supports what I just said:

> America is under attack from within. Our culture, our history, our founding are under the most direct assault I have seen in my life. And I'm sure it's the same with you. We haven't seen anything like this. You might even get away with saying that we are on the cusp of a second civil war. Some of you might say that we are already into it, that it has already begun. However you characterize it, though, we are under attack from within. And it's being bought and paid for by people from outside America, in addition to inside. If you're gonna defend the United States of America, you have to know our history. You have to know the purpose of the United States of America. You have to know unequivocally and proudly the United States' place in history. And that is why erasing and distorting our history is crucial for the left to succeed.

Limbaugh said he believes George Soros and other international financiers are continuously working toward the objective of destroying traditional American values in order to erase the United States as a powerful or super powerful nation. Without question, individual progressives and progressive organizations are orchestrating all the current upheaval in the U.S. and blaming traditional America as a flawed nation. Aldous Huxley once said, "The propagandist's purpose is to make one set of people forget that certain other sets of people are human."

I have read articles about Soros, reviewed Soros' website, and seen videos of Soros that support Limbaugh's opinion of him. I said in chapter 5 that Soros is a globalist who loves to ideologically and financially support the overthrow of governments. He has condemned the U.S. on several occasions. You will read later in the Epilogue that our own government under Obama has given Soros millions of dollars to support this kind of activity around the world. That's hard to believe but true. Why wouldn't the Obama administration give him money to eradicate traditional American ideology since that was the goal of our past president and many government officials in his administration?

What will "utopia America" be like under Marxist rule if the progressives win? Orwell's *1984* is a good place to start. America will become similar to Oceania. Oceania is a totalitarian dystopia controlled by the Inner Party. It is a country of perpetual government cover-up, widespread government surveillance, and government manipulation of society. Sounds like the Obama administration. The Ministry of Peace oversees war and defense. The Ministry of Plenty oversees economic affairs (rationing and starvation). The Ministry of Love oversees law and order (torture and brainwashing). Sounds like the current progressive movement. The Ministry of Truth oversees news, entertainment, education, and art (propaganda). Sounds like the progressives and their un-news media lap dogs. The controlling political party (the Inner Party) is not interested in the good of the people but seeks power for its own sake. It persecutes individualism and individual thinking. The government rewrites history so that historical records support the Inner Party's propaganda. Sounds like the progressives to me.

Does Oceania sound far-fetched for America? We are already far down the road. All one has to do is to look at the scandals discussed in the original book and outlined later in this Epilogue that are associated with the Obama administration. We were much closer than you might think during the eight years that Obama was president and the current shadow government is doing a magnificent job of continuing down that road in spite of the Trump pro-American presidency. Here are a few examples of current and past progressive behavior that fits the *1984* narrative:

- Restriction of free speech that is in opposition to progressive ideology; i.e., restriction of and violence against conservative speech on college campuses and elsewhere
- Practicing hypocrisy toward those who are in opposition: i.e., defending gay rights at the expense of restricting religious rights
- Ignoring the Constitution; i.e., ignoring the 1st and 2nd Amendments and ignoring or misinterpreting Constitutional laws that do not conform to progressive ideology
- Rewriting and restating history to support the progressive narrative; i.e., Civil War and slavery, historical global colonization, and historical American ideological culture
- Manipulation of society through lies and deception; i.e., Obamacare, racism, Benghazi, and the Iran deal
- No accountability for illegal actions by progressive government officials; i.e., Lois Learner, Eric Holder, Loretta Lynch, and Hillary Clinton
- Behavior and actions are for the benefit of progressives and not society as a whole; i.e., government policies and laws by the EPA, DOJ, etc. that restrict the freedoms of American citizens and increase government control and power
- Illegal spying to control political opponents and American citizens who oppose them; i.e., the Trump/Russia debacle, the AP and James Rosen affair, Sharyl Attkisson, the NSA scandal, and Federal Communications Commission (FCC) attempts to control public communication
- Using government agencies to control political opponents and to punish those in opposition to their progressive ideology; i.e., IRS and DOJ scandals
- Utilizing illegal voting and buying votes to obtain and preserve power; i.e., registering illegal immigrants and refugees, allowing

60

unverified voters, increasing food stamp and welfare recipients, unverified Obamacare subsidies, and unverified tax credit payments to low income citizens and non-citizens
- Using the federal court system to implement and preserve progressive ideology by not adhering to written and case law; i.e., immigration laws and Trump presidential directives that are contrary to progressive ideology
- Funding progressive anti-American organizations through government agencies; i.e., DOJ, EPA, and State Department funding radical progressive organizations within the U.S. and funding global government takeovers through George Soros' radical Open Society organization
- False and misleading progressive propaganda; mainstream news and entertainment media are extremely complicit in presenting a false narrative to the public supporting progressive ideology and demonizing the opposition

This is only a snapshot of what has occurred and is occurring. It is scary as hell when one puts it all together. We should never be so smug to think we can't eventually wind up like the Marxist-based countries I discussed throughout the original book and in this Epilogue that succumbed to progressive control and over time became increasingly more dystopian.

I often think how dystopian our country would become under progressive rule. The answer is somewhere beginning with the Western European countries and ending with Russia. Yes Russia! Look how dystopian we became under the Obama administration and are continuing to become because of current progressive ideological aggression. This is occurring even though President Trump is championing traditional American values to preserve our country's historical success.

The continued success of our American society depends upon governance being run like a business, not an ideological journey. Adherence to the principles and laws set forth in our founding documents is paramount and must be subject to change only by using those same principles and laws to do so. Governance by progressive whims of idealogical fanciful bliss is destructive and guarantees rule by manipulation and corruption.

There are many progressive organizations like Obama's OFA organization that promote, participate in, and fund anti-American behavior. This progressive activity receives significant endorsement and financial support from political and non-political entities and from public figures including the entertainment elite. Madonna wanting to blow up the White House and Ashley Judd's nasty women speech come to mind. How about stand-up comedian Kathy Griffin holding a simulated bloody severed head that looked like Trump's head? She received a backlash and apologized but only honestly expressed remorse after she was fired from: her advertising contract with Squatty Potty (yes, Squatty Potty); her remaining tour dates; and her upcoming New Years Eve appearance on CNN (yes, CNN fired her). These are the people who call Trump a loose cannon???

Our progressive friend, Mayor de Blasio, went to Hamburg, Germany during the G-20 protests to speak against the G-20 and President Trump. In chapter 4, it was learned that de Blasio was an active supporter of the communist Sandinista regime in Nicaragua during the 1980s. His trip to Hamburg was one day after a young female NYC police officer with three children was randomly shot and killed as she sat in her police vehicle. He also missed a swearing-in ceremony for 524 new police recruits. His trip did not play well in New York City or around the country and rightfully so. He did return home in time for the police officer's funeral and the NYC police at the funeral physically turned their backs on him—again.

How can people like de Blasio and other progressives think the way they do? Easy, because they are elitists and ordinary humans like us are their experimental palette to toy with and control. Always remember *The Nudge*. Progressives also find ways to embellish their personal lifestyle in contrast to what they philosophically preach; i.e., the Clinton-Russia uranium scandal. Isn't this scandal the kind of fascism that progressives speak out against? Isn't this extremely hypocritical? Yes and yes! What else is new? This is the world we have to look forward to if the progressives gain power and control in perpetuity. It will be a combination of *1984* and *Animal Farm* that were discussed in chapter 13. Interestingly, George Orwell wrote both books.

I have no doubt the Steele intelligence report and other nefarious intelligence gathering activity by the Obama administration was a well-orchestrated effort to develop the Russian collusion narrative to condemn Trump, provide an ongoing basis to delegitimize his presidency, and support his potential impeachment. This is the path progressives chose to destroy their competition to regain power. If they gain control in perpetuity, what would they do to you if you opposed them? The IRS scandal would be a good example. Scary, isn't it?

One of the most talked about events regarding Russian collusion involves a Trump Jr., Paul Manafort, and Jared Kushner meeting with a Russian attorney during the presidential campaign. The person who set up the meeting was a prior business acquaintance of President Trump. The acquaintance said the Russian attorney had damning information on Hillary. The meeting apparently turned out to be a ruse to discuss the Magnitsky Act, which is legislation passed by Congress to punish Russia for Sergei Magnitsky's death. Magnitsky mysteriously died in a Russian prison after his investigation of Russian fraud. In retaliation of the act, Russia stopped the ability of our citizens to adopt Russian children.

Kushner and Manafort left the meeting early and Trump Jr. said the meeting was a bust. The news media and progressive politicians have milked this event for all they can. I wish the news media had even one one-hundredth of the same level of interest in the Clinton-Russia uranium scandal. The initial email to Trump Jr. was written very carefully to acknowledge that a person associated with the Russian government was involved in obtaining the information on Hillary. Trump Jr. said he considered the meeting to be opposition research and was not concerned because the Russian collusion narrative was not in existence at that time.

It is worth noting that Guy Benson wrote a Townhall article in August about a story in the Washington Post that has received very little news media attention. The Post article said email records were discovered that show a Trump low level campaign volunteer with little foreign policy experience persisted that Trump or members of his team meet with Russian officials during the election and was repeatedly rebuffed. Benson said, "These freshly-revealed emails look like a conscience campaign doing the right thing and expressing appropriate skepticism when approached about opportunities to huddle with the Russians."

Magnitsky's business partner was scheduled to appear before the Senate Judiciary Committee to testify that the Trump Jr. meeting was a ruse to discuss the Magnitsky Act and involved our friends at Fusion GPS. The democrats invoked the same rule to stop this testimony they used to stop the hearing on unmasking. I thought the democrats wanted to uncover the truth about Russian collusion? Only if it hurts the Trump administration and does not uncover any covert action by progressives against Trump and his associates!

Could the Obama administration have been monitoring the Trump political organization through government intelligence gathering? Could the Obama administration have built the Russia scandal narrative from the Fusion GPS Trump dossier and by monitoring meetings such as the Magnitsky meeting? Could the Magnitsky meeting have been a conspiracy that was set up by progressives such as the DNC, the Clinton Campaign, and perhaps the Obama administration for later use as part of a contrived Russian collusion scandal? Great questions! I would say yes to all three!

The person who set up the meeting with Trump Jr. is British as is Christopher Steele. The Russian attorney involved in the meeting is connected to Fusion GPS as is Steele. Remember, Fusion GPS is an opposition research firm that has connections to the DNC and the Clinton campaign. We do not know who else. I might also add that the Russian attorney had to get a special visa to enter the U.S. from the Obama administration. Who knows what the real truth is but I smell a rat in here somewhere and it's not Trump Jr.

A recent news report by the Fox News staff uncovered a smear campaign against a London-based news reporter (Hmm? Here is a London connection again.) who exposed corruption between the late

Venezuelan dictator Hugo Chavez and a Venezuelan power company, which was one of Fusion GPS's clients. The London reporter said two computers were stolen from his apartment that contained information about the Venezuelan scandal and afterwards the Venezuelan intelligence police attacked his sources. His children were anonymously threatened and he was anonymously smeared on the Internet as a pedophile, drug addict, and a thief. A Venezuelan human rights activist testified before Congress that Fusion GPS had "smear experts" and used "scorched earth methods". The Venezuelan power company and Fusion GPS refused comment. No surprise there!

I find it very interesting that it has been widely reported the Obama administration, including Obama himself, knew about the Russian interference in our presidential election at least two months before our government took any action and then the action was minimal. Apparently, action was taken only after the administration received letters from democratic Senators Feinstein and Cardin urging them to do so. Politico reported Obama knew in 2014 the Russian's were meddling in our elections and did nothing because he did not want to anger them.

Obama's Homeland Security Secretary, Jeh Johnson, testified before Congress that he offered assistance to the DNC after learning they were being hacked and his offer was declined. Why didn't the Obama administration or the DNC take action to stop the Russians if this was such a serious intrusion into our election process? Very strange and raises lot's of questions. Was the DNC hiding something they did not want anyone outside the organization to know about? The more one digs into this, the stronger that rat smells.

Politico reported during the Trump Jr. controversy that a DNC operative met with Ukrainian government officials and received negative information regarding Paul Manafort in order to help Hillary's campaign. This was said to be the reason for Manafort's resignation as Trump's campaign manager. The FBI raided Manafort's home in July and he has been indicted. It appears Manafort did participate in illegal activity that had nothing to do with the Trump campaign. Where is this indictment going and why? Is it just to put a trophy head on the wall to justify Mueller spending $6.7 million as of December in his investigation and the DOJ spending another $3.5 million to support it?

The progressives and their supportive news media said the Ukraine situation is different from the Trump Jr. meeting because Russia is a hostile government and an enemy of the U.S. Really? Then, why did Hillary push a reset button with Russia in 2009 and in 2012 Obama send a message to Putin that he would have more flexibility after his reelection? Which is it with Russia? Progressives always want it both ways depending upon their motives.

The progressives added another wrinkle in their quest to destroy President Trump by accusing him of obstruction of justice resulting from his interactions with Comey. The progressives constantly look for anything including false narratives in their quest to vilify Trump. I have heard many attorneys who are knowledgeable in such matters (even a well known staunch liberal attorney) say there is absolutely no case for obstruction of justice. Unfortunately, these accusations keep the negativity front and center in the public eye to taint Trump as a bad and corrupt president.

One of the latest efforts by the progressives and the news media to vilify Trump involves General Flynn's guilty plea as a result of the Mueller Russia investigation. Flynn pleaded guilty that he lied to the FBI about his conservations with the Russian ambassador after Trump won the election. The progressives and the news media have tried to use Flynn's plea to report that Trump did something wrong, which is totally false. Is Flynn another trophy head for the wall?

The chief investigative reporter for ABC was given four weeks leave without pay because of his irresponsible and false reporting against Trump as a result of the Flynn plea. Flynn was out of money for attorney fees and faced about 60 years in jail for other illegalities he was being investigated for that had nothing to do with Trump. His son was also in jeopardy of legal action. A guilty plea that will net him six to twelve months in jail, keep his son out of jail, and negate attorney fees is a great trade off.

I find it interesting that the judge who was involved in Flynn's plea was appointed by Obama and has recused himself from Flynn's sentencing. It is suspected that the judge did so because he is also on the FISA court. This could be another interesting development as it plays out.

The midterm elections are only eleven months away and all 435 seats in the House and 33 of the 100 seats in the Senate are up for grabs. The stakes are high for both parties. The progressives will do whatever they believe they need to do to gain control of the House, Senate, and White House. That includes the dishonest destruction of the Trump administration and any calamitous effects that would have on America or the American people. They really care about us American citizens, don't they?

It has been reported that progressives and progressive organizations (many of which I talked about in the original book) are being led by George Soros and Media Matters founder David Brock to raise $40 million during 2017 to impeach President Trump. The effort's centralized hub is ImpeachDonaldTrumpNow.org and is led by two groups. They are called Free Speech for People and RootsAction. Their website says, "The nation is now witnessing a massive corruption of the presidency, far worse than Watergate."

One of their fellow progressive groups called Citizens for Responsibility and Ethics in Washington (CREW) filed a lawsuit in late May saying that Trump was in violation of the Emoluments Clause because he did not not adequately divest himself of his real estate holdings in countries outside the U.S. I commented in chapter 8 that the names of these progressive organizations are always the opposite of reality; i.e., free speech, responsibility, ethics, etc.? The lawsuit is said to be without merit or standing and will go nowhere. The attorneys general from the District of Columbia and Maryland sued trump in June for the same reason. Both are democrats and you can bet they are progressives. Most recently, six House democrats have called for impeachment hearings. This is further evidence that these progressives work in unison to destroy the Trump presidency. The CREW website says:

Donald Trump spoke often during the presidential campaign to "drain the swamp"—that is, to clean up the corruption, influence, and cronyism that is too prevalent in Washington. Unfortunately, the first 100 days of the Trump administration has had precisely the opposite effect, bringing in conflicts of interest and ethical and legal problems on a massive scale not seen since at least President Nixon and perhaps ever.

There is zero proof that president Trump or anyone associated with him did anything wrong involving collusion with Russia, obstruction of justice, or anything illegal before or after the election. This is after massive illegal leaks to the press that have been enormous smoke but absolutely no fire. I strongly believe, with all the leaking going on, we would have learned about anything incriminating by now if there was anything of substance. Nothing we have heard regarding Trump, his campaign team, or his administrative team even comes close to being as concerning as when Obama did not know his microphone was on and told then Russian president, Dmitry Medvedev, to tell Putin that it was his last term and he would have more flexibility after the 2012 election. What the hell did that mean? No one, including the news media, was concerned enough to attempt to find out.

I heard Ari Fleischer (press secretary under George Bush) say on Fox News, "Knowing Washington, if there was any guilt, it would have been leaked." Even Comey's testimony before Congress did not produce anything to indicate that President Trump or anyone else in his administration did anything illegal or unethical and Comey said Trump was not under investigation. The continuous supposedly incriminating accusations toward Trump by the progressives and the mainstream news media are nothing more than what any other president has done and are perfectly legal according to trusted legal analysts.

I often wonder what Trump's behavior would be like if he were not under constant attack by the press and his progressive enemies. The impulsive behavior he often exhibits in his Tweets, personal comments, and personal actions would continue but not as frequently and defensively because he would not feel that he has to constantly defend himself.

Are you as tired as I am of hearing Representative Maxine Watters calling for Trump's impeachment in her loudmouth unprofessional manner? Did you know that The Citizens for Responsibility and Ethics in Washington cited Watters as the most corrupt Washington politician in 2005, 2006, 2009, and 2011 according to theblaze and other reports? It was also reported that she was charged with three counts of violating House ethics rules in 2010 for helping a bank in which her husband owned stock secure a federal bailout. How is she still in Office???

The hypocrisy among progressive politicians such as Watters is staggering. I heard the other day that Watters had thoughts of running for president. I cannot think of words to express my opinion on that one. Maybe she and Elizabeth Warren could run together in 2020 as president and vice president. Can you imagine watching those two go after each other to determine which one would be the candidate for president? It would be "last woman standing".

Speaking of attacks on President Trump, let's revisit the comments made by the progressive organizations that are trying to impeach him. They said Trump is a massive corruption of the presidency, far worse than Watergate, and has brought conflicts of interest and ethical and legal problems on a massive scale not seen since at least President Nixon and perhaps ever. Let's see how these accusations stack up to our last president and their progressive hero, Barrack Obama. I have reviewed below some of the scandals during the Obama administration that were discussed in the original book and declared to be "phony" by President Obama. I also added a few more recent discoveries.

- Obamacare: Americans were lied to about keeping their doctors and their insurance coverage in order to implement a government controlled health insurance plan that was in reality a tax on all Americans to fund a new welfare program for uninsured Americans. Obamacare was never going to work as presented and is a Trojan horse designed to force conversion to national healthcare.

- Benghazi: One of the worst and saddest cover-ups in our country's history. A terrorist attack on one of our embassies killed the ambassador and three others. The White House and Hillary covered up the fact that it was a terrorist attack and available military help was not sent to counter the attackers. Obama's re-election was three months away and he had declared that Osama bin Laden was dead and ISIS was a JV team. Hillary was going to run for president and did not want this terrorist attack on her record.

- Hillary Clinton Email Scandal: Hillary used a private email server for government correspondence that included highly classified information, which is illegal. The DOJ, under Loretta Lynch, did not prosecute her even though there was overwhelming evidence of guilt. James Comey verbally indicted Hillary on national television but said no one would prosecute her because intent could not be proven. Even though intent was blatantly obvious, the law does not require intent for prosecution. Obama was said to have known about her private server. Lynch met privately with Bill Clinton prior to Comey's comments. Comey stated before Congress that Lynch asked him to publicly call the investigation a "matter" as used by Hillary's campaign and not call it an "investigation". It has been suggested there was collusion between Obama and Lynch to shut down the investigation because Obama would have been implicated since he was a knowing participant who sent and received emails on Hillary's private server. I read this would be a felony and impeachable offense for Obama. It has also been suggested that Bill threatened Lynch during their meeting that Hillary would expose this fact under oath if the DOJ pursued indictment. In any case, this is blatant political corruption. The Senate Judiciary Committee reopened the investigation because of recent congressional testimony by Comey regarding Lynch's directive and the discovery that Comey drafted the document exonerating Hillary two months before her and her staffs' interviews by the FBI. Retired Intelligence Community Inspector General Charles McCullough III recently told Fox News the Clinton emails contained 2100 classified emails including 22 that were top secret. He said he reported this to James Clapper, Director of National Intelligence, and to the Senate Intelligence and Foreign Relations committees. Clapper said it was extremely reckless. Democratic congressional members and senior Obama officials threatened McCullough. Officials from the Clinton campaign told him and a colleague in the matter they would be the first two to be fired after Hillary was elected. He said if he had done what Hillary did he would be in Leavenworth. It has also recently been reported that the top FBI agent assigned to Mueller's Russia investigation was reassigned because he was caught exchanging text messages with his mistress, who also works at the FBI, which expressed a multitude of political opinions critical of Trump. His messages included calling Trump an "idiot", saying the Republican Party "needs to pull their head out of their ass", and said Bernie Sanders is "an idiot like Trump". This is the FBI agent that led the FBI's investigation of Hillary's private email server and changed the wording on Comey's exoneration of Clinton. There are others on Mueller's investigative team that have connections to the Clinton Foundation, have donated money to Hillary's campaign and other democratic election funds, and are known to be sympathetic to progressive ideology. This gives me more than casual concern that Mueller's investigation is not objective and honest and is a part of the progressive shadow government witch-hunt against the Trump presidency. I have my fingers crossed that justice may prevail regarding Hillary's email and pay-to-play foundation scandals but I will not hold my breath. Hillary has never been prosecuted during the multiple times during her life that she has been investigated for criminal activity.

- Clinton Foundation: The Clintons made hundreds of millions of dollars providing favors to individuals and foreign countries during Hillary's position as Secretary of State and Bill being a past U.S. president. For example, they were involved in a deal that provided Russia roughly 50% of the world's supply of weapons' grade uranium. Approximately 20% came from the U.S. It is being reported that the Clinton foundation received a total of $145 million from those involved. Bill received a $500,000 speaker's fee from a Russian investment bank that was involved. Illegal activity like this answers why she used a private server to cover up her and her staff's actions.
- Illegal spying on news media: The DOJ illegally obtained telephone records of AP reporters and James Rosen of Fox News in an effort to determine the origin of leaks unflattering to the administration. When this illegal activity became public, Obama asked Eric Holder to investigate himself, which he did and declared he had solved everything with the news media.
- Fast and Furious: The DOJ made every effort to cover up their failed attempt to sell guns to drug dealers and trace their distribution in order to obtain information on the drug cartels' leaders. One of the guns was used to kill one of our U.S. Border Patrol agents and many of the guns were used to kill innocent Mexican citizens. Eric Holder was held in contempt of Congress due to his and the DOJ's lack of cooperation and Holder's false testimony before Congress. Nothing ever happened.
- Operation Choke Point: The program was started by the DOJ in order to provide the Obama administration the ability to make moral judgments against legitimate businesses they deemed to be undesirable. The program used the FDIC to pressure banks to not work with the businesses that were targeted. The two businesses that seemed to be most targeted were those dealing in short-term and payday loans and to gun and ammunition stores. No surprise on that last one.
- IRS Scandal: As bad as all these scandals are, this scandal and Benghazi are at the top of my list. It is unthinkable that our

own government would use the IRS to intimidate and punish American citizens who were deemed to be political opposition. There is also evidence that the IRS was working with the DOJ before the scandal was exposed to punish the identified citizens through the legal system. I wrote about a woman in chapter 9 who was president of a Tea Party organization and under scrutiny by the IRS. The IRS, the FBI, the Bureau of Alcohol, Tobacco, Firearms and Explosives (ATF), and the EPA investigated the business she owned with her husband. Obama said during an interview with Bill O'Reilly, "People (at the IRS) made some bone-headed decisions but there was not one smidgeon of corruption". The whole thing was shoved under the rug by the Obama administration. It is hard to believe this could happen in America. I feel mystified and extremely troubled every time I think of this abuse of power and the travesty of injustice by Obama's progressive government.

- National Security Agency Scandal: Edward Snowden exposed the excessive spying on Americans by the NSA. I watched the Director of National Intelligence, James Clapper, lie to Congress during a hearing on the issue. I discussed in chapter 8 the enormous data center that was built in Utah during the Obama administration that is capable of tracking and storing "all" forms of personal communication on "all" Americans. Why? To identify and spy on political dissenters or anyone else they wish to spy on?

- Federal Communications Commission Scandal: I discussed in chapter 5 the White House Czar under Obama who became a top official at the FCC and said freedom of speech was a distraction. He said he was personally opposed to private control of the media. This Czar also praised Chávez for knowing how to control the media to win revolutions. The Obama administration attempted to utilize the FCC more than once to shut down conservative speech. One attempt was a scam called the Multi-Market Study of Critical Information Needs that I discussed in chapter 6. There were also efforts to have the FCC control the Internet through net neutrality.

- Surveillance of Sharyl Attkisson: Obama's controversial advisor, Ben Rhodes, is the brother of the CEO at CBS News. Attkisson worked for CBS News for over 20 years. She wrote several news stories that were critical of the Obama administration and CBS started to retract her stories from being published. In addition, she believed her computers were being monitored at work and at home by the DOJ. On one occasion she watched her home computer rapidly erase all of the information stored on it. She later found three classified government documents on her computer that did not belong to her and could have gotten her in serious trouble. A security expert told her he found proof that her computer and her house had been electronically monitored by a government agency. She resigned from CBS, testified before Congress regarding what happened, and sued the DOJ and Eric Holder to no avail. She has appealed.

- The Bergdahl Debacle: Bowe Bergdahl was an Army deserter who was captured by the Taliban. Obama traded five top Taliban prisoners from Gitmo to obtain his release. There was suspicion a monetary ransom was also paid. The trade was a ruse by Obama to circumvent Congress in releasing Gitmo prisoners as he attempted to close Gitmo. There was also suspicion that Obama used this event to divert negative reaction regarding the Veterans Affairs healthcare scandals. The outcome of Bergdahl's trial was conveniently deferred until after Obama left office. Bergdahl finally pleaded guilty to desertion and misbehavior before the enemy. Stunningly, he recently received only a dishonorable discharge. He could have and should have spent the rest of his life in prison.

- Illegal Voting: Studies have been reported that indicate there are between 600,000 and 6 million illegal votes by non-residents, people voting in more than one state, and people who are deceased. No matter what the actual number is, it is significant. It explains why progressives who foster illegal voting are so strongly against effective voter verification. I wrote about The Election Assistance Commission in chapter 8, which is a small independent agency of the federal government that approves all state voter registration forms. The agency has historically denied any changes to any state voter registration form that could be used to identify illegal voters. Illegal voting proliferated under Obama administration policies.

- Manipulation of educational institutions: Federal grants and Title IX were used to coerce educational institutions to adopt progressive ideology by threatening to stop federal funding if they did not comply.

- Israel Election Influence: There was evidence discussed in chapter 7 that indicated the Obama administration provided millions of dollars and political operatives to attempt the defeat of Prime Minister Netanyahu in his last election. How hypocritical is that? United States election scandal vs. Russia election scandal—take your pick.

- Funding George Soros' Open Society: Not only was the Obama administration accused of meddling in Israel's election, they have funded George Soros' Open Society Foundation efforts around the world by millions of dollars to affect regime change. No one really knows the extent of this funding. The Daily Signal reported the U.S. Agency for International Development (USAID) has given approximately $5 million to the Open Society Institute to overthrow the Macedonian government and support a coalition that is composed of communists and Islamic supporters. I keep reading that Soros fights communism around the world through his Open Society. It doesn't sound like it. It sounds like a ruse to hide his real intentions. The takeover of Macedonia would result in the demise of a government that is strongly pro-American and pro-capitalism. The Daily Signal also reported USAID has given millions to Soros' Open Society in multiple countries around the globe to help promote his radical ideology that includes open international borders, one global government, legalized abortion, decriminalization of drugs, legalized prostitution, transgender rights, climate change, and radicalism in general. Have you ever heard of another Soros international organization funded by USAID called the Organized Crime and Corruption Reporting Project? I said to be careful of progressive names for organizations. This organization is targeting conservative politicians and conservative think tanks that are exposing USAID's funding of Soros' radical projects. Republican Senators sent a letter to Secretary of State Rex Tillerson asking this practice by USAID be investigated for "pushing a world wide progressive agenda and invigorating the left". Conservative House members have inquired to the State Department about the subject as well. Obama holdovers have thus far thwarted all of their efforts. This raises an interesting question. Is the progressive movement in America part of an effort to implement Marxist ideology throughout the world using affiliated organizations like Soros' Open Society? Far fetched? No! The more I study this issue the more I believe it could be true and scary as hell. It's like a James Bond movie where an international based syndicate like Spectre wants to politically manipulate the world and model it after *1984*. We know about Soros and his international political activities. I wonder who besides Soros could be a silent leader in the international progressive movement? I find it impossible to believe Soros is the only one. Knowing who all the players are could be extremely interesting and extremely troubling.

- Funding Radical Organizations: In addition to Soros' Open Society, the Obama administration used the DOJ, EPA, State Department, and other branches of government to channel billions of dollars to radical groups inside and outside the U.S. and avoid congressional oversight. For example, the DOJ incentivized financial institutions and businesses to pay a significant portion of their government fines to radical social justice organizations and progressive causes such as the National Council of La Raza and the National Urban League. It has been reported that $3 billion has been identified thus far as being paid to radical organizations like these two. Judicial Watch President Tom Fitton said, "It's a shakedown. It's corrupt, pure and simple." The State Department paid the second $500 million payment of Obama's promised $3 billion payment to the U.N. Green Climate Fund for the Paris climate accord in January as he left office. The AP reported the Obama administration gave out millions of dollars to left-wing causes just hours before he left office including $221 million to the Palestinian Authority. Palestinian Authority??? My research indicates that funneling money to radical organizations through various government departments was a common practice during the Obama era. No wonder radicals get upset when progressives are ousted from office. Their government support and funding is negatively affected. And, no wonder progressive politicians support these radical groups when these radical groups support progressive ideological endeavors and return a significant amount of their government funding to the progressive politicians' campaign coffers. Think Planned Parenthood. The Trump administration is in the process of putting a stop to this practice. I wrote extensively in chapter 10 about Planned Parenthood funding and the illegal sale of baby parts from aborted fetuses. It has recently been reported that the FBI is finally looking into their practice of selling baby parts for profit. This would never have happened under Obama and didn't.

- Ideologically Corrupt Federal Judges: During Obama's presidency, he appointed some of the most liberal, ideological, and radical judges to ever sit on the federal bench according to The Heritage Foundation. Even The New York Times said court cases would "end up before more ideologically sympathetic judges". Obama appointed two Supreme Court Justices, 329 federal judges with lifetime appointments representing almost 40% of the entire federal judiciary, and shifted nine of the thirteen circuit appeals courts to the left. We have seen the outcome of those appointments during the first months of the Trump presidency (the travel ban controversy for example) and will for decades to come. Where the Obama appointments have occurred, decisions based upon progressive ideology have replaced decisions based upon written law, case law, objectivity, and the Constitution. It gives a whole new look to Lady Justice. Instead of a blindfold, she now wears progressive eyeglasses (pun intended). Her scale that balanced the strengths of "support and opposition" is now held much further left from her body and modified with ideological weights. Her sword that designates authority is now raised high in the air to designate victory rather than to designate that justice will be swift and final. Her toga that represented justice has been stripped from her body and dropped to the ground. She is now naked and exposed but not to the truth.

- Iran Nuclear Deal: This is a scandalous blunder by Obama that materially impacts our national security. Ben Rhodes publicly admitted that the White House lied to the news media and the American people about the Iran deal. We gave Iran between $1.7 and $33.6 billion (no one really knows) in cash and reportedly in gold and other precious metals to buy Iran's signatures on a totally one-sided agreement and pay ransom for U.S. citizens. We have historically not paid ransom to rogue countries to avoid encouraging the kidnaping of Americans. Why was the payment to Iran done in a manner that was untraceable? Good question! Could some of the money have wound up in Iranian leaders' pockets? I'll let your imagination answer that one. What did American citizens get for the payment? We got an unabated future nuclear threat from a country that chanted "death to America" during negotiations and continues to do so today. What did Iran get? Beaucoup money up front, the ability to generate increased funding for terrorism, lax nuclear weapons oversight by the international community, and free reign to cheat on the agreement. Col. Oliver North of Fox News said something interesting. He commented that North Korea received a portion of our payment to Iran for their anti-American nuclear missile program. What did Obama get? A presidential legacy of throwing the U.S. and some of our closest allies under the bus. The Obama administration was so tough during the negotiations that Iran was only allowed to receive $700 million per month from funds previously frozen by U.S.

sanctions during the 17 months it took to finalize and sign the deal. Don't forget they also protected members of Hezbollah from prosecution by the DEA for smuggling cocaine into the U.S. and then shut down the entire investigation once the Iran deal was signed.

Now that we have taken a look at some of the major Obama administration scandals, let's look at Trump administration scandals. Hmm, I can't think of any! Can you? It appears to me that it is Obama (not Trump) who is a massive corruption of the presidency far worse than Watergate and brought conflicts of interest, ethical issues, and legal problems on a massive scale not seen since at least President Nixon and perhaps ever.

It was discussed in chapter 6 that the mainstream news media ignored or grossly under-reported Obama scandals when he was in office and they are continuing to do so today. We have already discussed the lack of coverage regarding new information on Hillary and Bill Clinton's Russian uranium scandal. Another recent example is the Circa News report implicating the Obama administration in spying on American citizens including the Trump campaign team. Fox News' James Rosen reported that CBS, NBC, ABC, The New York Times, and The Washington Post totally ignored the scathing report by Circa News.

Mainstream news also took a leave of absence regarding the recent announcement by the Senate Judiciary Committee that they are revisiting Loretta Lynch's actions during the Hillary Clinton investigation. Fox News reported the story over a two-day period. ABC reported the story for 31 seconds. NBC and CBS did not report the story at all. At the same time, the news media can't report enough, without any proof whatsoever, on alleged Trump scandals and blunders. Fox News said during the two-day period surrounding the Loretta Lynch issue that Trump-Russia news was aired 14 minutes and 22 seconds on ABC, 11 minutes and 42 seconds on NBC, and 19 minutes and 9 seconds on CBS.

Besides the continuous Trump scandal reporting, we consistently hear from the news media that Trump is not keeping his campaign promises and is not getting anything done. Let's take a look at what has been accomplished as of November in spite of the lack of cooperation and the obstructionist attitude exhibited by progressives and the news media:

- Illegal immigration on our southern border is down 70% due to tougher border control and enforcing immigration laws. Fox News reported that when Phoenix suspended their sanctuary city policies the murder rate fell 27%, robberies fell 23%, assaults fell 13%, burglaries fell 14%, and theft fell 19%. In the face of progressive pushback, the person reporting these statistics stood by their assertion that the drop in crime was a result of suspending sanctuary city policies and not some other reason. Unfortunately, Phoenix reinstated sanctuary city policies in August after coming under pressure by radical groups. I find it surprising and unconscionable that Texas cities like Dallas and Austin are fighting to remain sanctuary cities when the Texas Department of Public Safety reported that between 2008 and 2014 criminal aliens committed over 600,000 crimes in the state, including approximately 3,000 murders. Attorney General Jeff Sessions is gearing up to withhold federal funding to sanctuary cities that break federal immigration law and these cities are already fighting back.
- Trump aggressively pursued and is still pursuing the repeal and replacement of Obamacare in the face of stiff opposition from democrats and unfortunately some republicans as well. He has rescinded by executive order the Obama mandate requiring employers and insurers to offer contraception coverage. Employers can now exempt themselves based upon religious or moral grounds. The ACLU has sued. I thought they were for the rights of all Americans. I guess they forgot about the 1st Amendment and believe religion and moral judgment are not personal rights. Trump has also stopped government payments to insurance companies. He is taking Obamacare apart piece

by piece with his pen as Obama patched its failures with his. Congress did omit the Obamacare individual mandate in the tax reform bill; however, the republican approach so far to resolve Obamacare is a total political cop-out and will not work to solve the problems it has created. It goes back to what I said in chapter 12 about many republicans putting their political future above serving the best interests of those who elected them. Unless this changes, the midterm elections could be disastrous for republicans.

- Trump pursued and accomplished tax reform. The republicans passed a tax reform bill without a single democratic vote. There was significant concern that a similar result might occur as it did with Obamacare and would have been a disaster for republicans in the midterm elections. Legendary Democratic Speaker of the House, Sam Rayburn, once said, "A jackass can kick down a barn but it takes a carpenter to build one." Even though the jackass is the symbol of his party, he was referring to the republicans when the democrats lost power in 1953. Well, the jackasses (progressive democrats) tore down the American barn for eight years and it's time for the republicans to become carpenters. Unfortunately, except for the tax reform bill, the republicans have hammered each other in the head instead of hitting the nail on the head. How sad when republicans have had so much opportunity. The repeal of Obamacare for example! The passage of the tax reform bill does provide hope for the republicans to keep the House and Senate after the midterm elections but they still have a lot of work to do to ensure they do.

- Trump's famous wall on the Mexican border is under design and money in the 2017 budget will be used to get the project started prior to pursuing final funding in the 2019 budget. He has said it will be a combination of an actual wall and other surveillance means.

- During Trump's first ten months, he signed 105 executive orders, memoranda, and determinations including the approval of the

Keystone XL Pipeline. He also signed 110 proclamations. Many of these actions got rid of an enormous number of Marxist ideologically based regulations and policies implemented by the Obama administration that stymied economic growth and infringed upon citizens rights; i.e., EPA environmental and Dodd-Frank banking regulations.

- Trump signaled a reversal of Obama's social justice war on religion by signing an executive order stating, "Federal law protects the freedom of Americans and their organizations to exercise religion and participate fully in civic life without undo interference by the Federal Government." Trump also spoke at a recent Family Research Council conference and stated, "Well guess what? We're saying 'Merry Christmas' again."
- Economic optimism has been high since Trump was elected as reflected by the stock market, unemployment numbers, and economic indexes that continuously hit new highs. GDP growth as of the third quarter has hit 3% two straight quarters.
- The U.S. Labor Department reported for the first time in years, workers at the lowest 10% level of wages outpaced the wage increases of the other 90%. The reason given by experts was the labor market is tightening because people have more disposable income to spend on restaurants, entertainment, and other businesses that depend upon lower paying jobs. This increase in business results in higher wages to attract employees. Minimum wage increases were also mentioned as a possibility but I discussed in chapter 8 that significantly higher unemployment resulted in all the cities I studied, which implemented minimum wage increases. Government regulation can never replace the success of free market capitalism.
- Trump's rhetoric and actions have increased consumer confidence, improved the economy, and created jobs. The U.S. Manufacturing Index is at a 33 year high, the highest since President Reagan.
- Trump has started discussions with Mexico, Canada, China, European countries, and others to improve our trade deficit and

to make our trade agreements more equitable. He also pulled out of the inequitable Trans-Pacific Partnership.

- NATO announced that member countries increased their funding by approximately $10 billion after Trump chastised the majority of members for not honoring their commitment to allocate 2% of GDP toward military spending. I read in The Wall Street Journal that Germany was so remiss in their NATO commitment that one of their infantry battalions complained they didn't have enough munitions to simulate battle so the soldiers were told to "imagine the bangs".

- Trump took us out of the horrendous Paris climate accord that required the U.S. (number two in the world's carbon output) to decrease carbon output much more aggressively than any other country in the world even though we were already far ahead of the others in our efforts. We were also required to pay hundreds of billions of dollars to developing countries to offset their cost to participate. This meant we would give hundreds of billions of dollars more than we currently give to developing countries and I'm sure a significant amount of that money would wind up in dishonest political leaders' personal bank accounts. The commitment of China (number one in carbon output) to the Paris accord was weak at best and a non-commitment at worst. India (number three in carbon output) said they would try.

- Neil Gorsuch was nominated and confirmed as the newest Supreme Court Justice. Gorsuch has a reputation of being an honest, pragmatic, and non-ideological judge in his decisions. He has proven himself to be a strong constitutionalist after becoming a member of the Court. Supreme Court Justices are crucial in upholding the Constitution and its American values. President Trump could have other opportunities—Justice Ginsburg is 84, Justice Kennedy is 81, and Justice Breyer is 79.

- Jerome Powell was chosen to replace Janet Yellen as Chairman of the Federal Reserve. Powell is a conservative and has been a very respected member of the Federal Reserve Board since 2012.

- The Trump administration is making serious efforts to solve the VA hospital patient scandal issues; i.e., the bipartisan VA Accountability and Whistleblower Protection Act. It was reported that more than 500 employees have been fired and 200 have been suspended. Those that were disciplined included 22 senior leaders, 70+ nurses, 14 police officers, and 25 physicians. That is certainly new! I have read that other federal government departments like the State Department are experiencing the same scrutiny as well as being downsized. These changes are long overdue. Not surprisingly, these actions are not going over well. The federal government is a big, deep, and nasty swamp and the creatures in that swamp do not give up without striking back as we have seen repeatedly.
- Trump's cabinet and other high level positions are being filled with very competent and conservative minded people.
- Trump's trips to Saudi Arabia, Israel, Brussels, Italy, France, and Asia have put the U.S. back on the map as the world leader in international relations.
- Trump's trip to Poland and the G-20 meeting was very successful. He was very presidential and he and his cabinet members who were in attendance were very well prepared.
- The Trump administration is rebuilding and modernizing our military, which has significantly decayed over the last eight years. We have abandoned Obama's position of "strategic patience" and are now taking a tough stand on Syria, Iran, North Korea, China, Russia, and terrorism. We are actively pushing back against Russia's aggressive taunting of the U.S. and our NATO allies and pushing back against China's aggression in the South China Sea. We are restoring our leadership position as the world's policeman and re-establishing our national security. We are back to "kicking ass" rather than "kissing ass" as I discussed in chapter 9.
- The Department of Justice, our top law body in the U.S., is in the process of re-establishing itself as an honest and effective government agency by working to omit the enormous political

corruption that infiltrated the agency during the Obama administration. The DOJ is improving in supporting the enforcement of laws throughout the country and supporting the law enforcement officers who enforce those laws. The DOJ is also tackling tough crime issues like MS-13.

- Trump revised our position with Cuba and rescinded Obama's policies that supported the repressive Cuban government and did not support Cuban citizen's rights.
- Trump has handled the crisis with North Korea magnificently contrary to what the news media reports. This is a very difficult situation at best and could have extremely serious ramifications. This issue started under Bill Clinton but proliferated under Bush and Obama.
- After Obama signed the disastrous deal with Iran, Congress passed a law titled the Iran Nuclear Review Act of 2015, which requires the president to certify Iran is complying with the provisions of the deal every ninety days. Trump refused to certify that Iran is in compliance. He stated Iran is not living up to the spirit of the deal and listed multiple violations. This triggered congressional action toward a tougher stance with Iran and puts Iran on notice that President Trump may get out of the deal altogether.
- The DOJ ended the unjust Operation Choke Point.
- The Trump administration got rid of net neutrality, which was deviously implemented by the Obama administration to control the Internet.
- Education Secretary Betsy DeVos rescinded the Obama administration's "guilty until proven innocent" guidance under Title IX that denied due process to male students accused of sexual assault on college campuses.
- Trump kept his campaign promise and declared Jerusalem the legitimate capital of Israel and announced the U.S. is going to move its embassy there from Tel Aviv. There was considerable criticism from the democrats and from leaders around the world. There is belief that much of the criticism by

world leaders is for political show rather than true criticism. Most of Israel's government is currently in Jerusalem. The U.S. Congress declared Jerusalem the capital in 1995. Presidents Clinton, Bush, and Obama said they would move our embassy to Jerusalem but did not.

- During October and November, refugee resettlement was down 83% from last year and the demographics of the refugees were more in line with successful assimilation into American culture.

We rarely hear about these accomplishments. Rarely! All we hear is negativity toward Trump and his administration and trumped up allegations (pun intended). For example, we consistently heard from the print media, television news, and Internet news that Trump fired Comey because of his investigation of Russia and the Trump campaign. I heard this almost daily for over a month.

I thought it was over until I surprisingly heard Chris Wallace of Fox News say it again not too long ago. I know he is not a fan of Trump but I was very surprised to hear Chris say that because it's not true. I have always thought of Chris as a very pragmatic and honest political commentator. I actually met him many years ago. I was very disappointed and concerned that even someone like Chris Wallace would jump on the anti-Trump bandwagon with a false narrative and send his pragmatism to the wind.

The source for the accusation is a May 11th Trump interview by Lester Holt on NBC News. It was obvious from Holt's questions that he wanted Trump to say he fired Comey because of the Russia investigation. In a relatively long interview, he prodded Trump several times in an effort to get him to admit that he did. Trump never said he fired Comey because of the Russia investigation.

I heard the accusation so often by the news media that I listened to the interview twice in its entirety to make sure I didn't miss anything. I even asked my wife to listen with me. Trump never said it. In fact, he said more than once during the interview that he did not fire Comey because of the Russia investigation. Taking Trump's comments out of context and concocting negative Trump stories is common occurrence for the news media in order to fabricate their desired news stories or as Trump calls it— "fake news".

The entire Trump administration is subject to "fake news". Here is a recent example. Senator James Lankford (R., OK.) wrote a letter to the president of ABC concerning a news report that Attorney General Jeff Sessions addressed members of the Alliance Defending Freedom, which had been designated an anti-LGBT hate group by the far-left SPLC. My research indicates that almost any group that does not adhere to progressive ideology is designated as a hate group by SPLC. The ABC headline read: "Jeff Sessions Addresses 'Anti-LGBT Hate Group' but DOJ Won't Release His Remarks." Sessions spoke on religious freedom.

Lankford's letter said, "… why would ABC News label a peaceful group as a 'hate group' simply because of a difference of opinion?" I have two answers for Senator Lankfort. First, it is classic "fake news" on the part of ABC. Secondly, the progressives routinely tout tolerance, understanding, and forgiveness but have zero tolerance, understanding, and forgiveness with anyone who has a difference of opinion with them. This phenomenon has increased significantly in intensity since Obama left office and the progressives' power has diminished.

I saw an interview recently on Fox and Friends with the Editor in Chief of The Knife Media. The firm rates news media regarding news bias. This is how they rated the following news organizations on objectivity in their reporting involving President Trump: CNN, 44.7%; The New York Times, 39.8%; and The Washington Post, 46.1%. They also rated the same news organizations on their reporting of news involving President Trump that was distorted by emotion rather than reporting the news factually: CNN, 62.9%; The New York Times, 62%; and The Washington Post, 61%.

A Rasmussen Poll taken in August of last year said 74% of likely voters felt the media was more interested in creating controversies about the candidates than where the candidates stood on issues. A Rasmussen poll taken in June of this year indicated 76% of GOP voters and 51% of independent voters believe most reporters are biased against Trump. A recent Harvard study revealed the same significant bias. The study showed the percent of reporting with a negative tone toward the president. The results were as follows: CNN at 93%; NBC at 93%; CBS at 91%; The New York Times at 87%; The Washington Post at 83%; The Wall Street Journal at 70%; and Fox News at 52%. Even the BBC was at 74%.

One could say the reason for all the negativity toward the Trump administration is because it is deserved. If you believed that, you would not be reading this Epilogue. A Quinnipiac University poll reported the following feelings of Americans toward the news media: 10% were enthusiastic; 30% were satisfied; 33% were dissatisfied; and 26% were angry.

Americans have great reason to be upset with the un-news media. It is not enough for some news organizations to put a negative spin on the news to push the progressive agenda. CNN either staged its own news story or knowingly participated in a staged news story to make the point they wanted to make. That is hard to believe but it is true. This situation is worse than the three contrived CNN News specials I discussed in chapter 9 that included Fareed Zakaria on Islamic terrorism, Katie Couric on gun control, and the one on college sexual assault. I saw the staging of this fake news story on cell phone videos taken by two different people who were in the vicinity.

CNN filmed interviews in London with a group of Muslim men, women, and children with signs and flowers in their hands who appeared to be demonstrating against the June 3rd Muslim attack at the London Bridge that killed eight people and injured 48 others. The news story presented by CNN (which I also watched) was that the Muslims who were interviewed were demonstrating to show they did not support jihad waged by Muslim extremists. It put Muslims in a very good light.

The cell phone videos showed the Muslims who were interviewed to be randomly milling around the area while CNN was setting up their cameras. They certainly were not demonstrating. They were then given professionally made signs and flowers by some unknown people and were carefully placed in front of the CNN cameras to be interviewed.

CNN denied the interview was staged and received support from the usual liberal media including Snopes, which claims to be the definitive fact-checking website. Whether CNN staged the protest themselves or participated in a staged protest, the outcome is the same. It is knowingly perpetrating false reporting.

CNN encountered three more hits on journalism ethics. They had to retract a news story and three journalists resigned because of a story on Anthony Scaramucci. Scaramucci was reported by CNN to have held a meeting with the head of a Russian investment firm prior to Trump's inauguration. Scaramucci was a Trump aide at the time and stated he only said a quick hello to the Russian in a restaurant. CNN said the story did not meet its standards and apologized to him.

Ironically, Scaramucci was named White House Director of Communications after this happened. Ironically again, Scaramucci went on a foul-mouthed rampage against Steve Bannon and Reince Priebus during an interview with The New Yorker and was fired after 10 days on the job by Trump's new chief of staff, John Kelly.

You are probably aware of the unknown individual who put a video on Reddit depicting President Trump beating-up the CNN logo. The man apologized to CNN and CNN reported they would keep the man's name confidential if he did not do anything against CNN again. CNN received severe criticism for threatening the individual with releasing his identity. I heard several attorneys say that CNN's actions could be considered coercion and illegal.

Here is a very damning story regarding CNN that was widely reported at the same time as the Scaramucci story. Veritas founder James O'Keefe interviewed a CNN producer on hidden camera. The CNN producer said the heavy coverage of collusion between Trump and Russia was "mostly bullshit". The Hill reported the producer said, "I just feel like they don't really have it, but they want to keep digging. And so I think the president is probably right to say, like, look you are witch hunting me." The producer was also quoted as saying, "All the nice little cutesy little ethics that used to get talked about in journalism school, you're just like, that's adorable." He continued, "That's adorable. This is business."

The producer commented the president of CNN said the following during an internal meeting, "… good job everybody covering the climate accords, but we're done with that, let's get back to Russia."

And, that they did. CNN has repeatedly been caught with their "fake news stories" as Trump continuously tweets.

Joe Scarborough's co-host and fiancée Mika Brzezinski on MSNBC's Morning Joe characterized it perfectly last February from a progressive narrative. She said:

> Well, I think that the dangerous, you know, edges here are that he (Trump) is trying to undermine the media and trying to make up his own facts. And it could be that while unemployment and the economy worsens, he could have undermined the messaging so much that he can actually control exactly what people think. And that, that is our job.

The "facts" are overwhelming that unemployment and the economy are improving, not worsening, and how about her position that it is the job of the news media to control what people think? As bizarre and troubling as Brzezinski's statement is, it speaks for the news media in general with the exception of the media that is conservative or leans conservative. I quoted John Adams, James Madison, Benjamin Franklin, Thomas Jefferson, and George Washington in chapter 6 regarding America remaining a free society and avoiding tyranny? They collectively said Americans must be truthfully and fully informed.

I also discussed the Sedona Observer Code of Ethics and the Code of Ethics for the Society of Professional Journalists in chapter 6. Each of these code of ethics strongly support what the founding fathers said regarding honest and thorough reporting. Oh, I forgot. Codes of ethics are adorable and the real world is business. I said in the original book that one of my favorite newspaper cartoon characters is Mallard Fillmore. He said, "If we media types were doing our job, both parties would regard us as 'The Opposition Party'."

The vast majority of news media with the exception of Fox News, conservative Internet websites, conservative radio shows, and a couple of newspapers is very progressive in its reporting and for the most part 100% unreliable. This is where most of America obtains its news and educates itself on America's political environment. I am such a pragmatist it drives me crazy. I do not understand how anyone can live and survive in such a cocoon of ideology-based existence when the real world is such a different place.

My local newspaper, like most news outlets, has become a progressive propaganda piece disguised as a newspaper. The distortion of the truth in the headlines and the articles themselves is unconstrained. I have learned to ignore the fake news and key on local news and the funnies. Well, at least most of the time. The daily political cartoons in the opinion section are the worst. All of the political cartoons, except one or two per month, are negative toward Trump and/or republicans. I recently read another one of Mallard Fillmore's cartoons in which he asked the media, "Media, can you explain the double standard in your 'political violence' coverage?" The media said, "Sure! Leftists are only being violent because they HATE TRUMP! So, it's ALL TRUMP'S FAULT!"

My local Gannett/USA TODAY owned newspaper started its own impeachment discussion in addition to ImpeachDonaldTrumpNow. org. There was an article on this morning's front page headlined "Poll: Americans split 42%-42% on impeaching Trump". There was also a picture of President Trump with a caption that said, "A USA TODAY/MediaEthics Poll found that 42 percent of voters support and the same percentage oppose removing President Donald Trump from office." All the quotes from people interviewed in the article were negative toward Trump and the last one said, "I believe in 2018 they will vote enough Democrats and independents in to impeach him." The front page of my local newspaper has become a new opinion page.

Actually, it appears that USA TODAY has taken this opinion page approach nationwide. A few weeks ago I was in Napa Valley, California. A USA TODAY newspaper on a newsstand in St. Helena had an article regarding Trump on the front page. The headline said "Trump Unhinged".

Speaking of being unhinged, the Vice President and Senior Council at CBS posted her thoughts on Facebook regarding the Las Vegas shooting massacre. She said, "If they wouldn't do anything when children were murdered, I have no hope the Repugs [*sic*] will ever do the right thing. I'm actually not even sympathetic (because) country music fans often are Republican gun toters." It takes a peculiar mindset to be capable of such a demented thought. After strong negative reaction, she was immediately fired by CBS after one year on the job.

Because of her lofty position in the organization, my guess is that CBS was very aware of her progressive ideology. I am not suggesting that CBS supported or agreed with her comments but I wonder what they would have done if there was not such a strong negative public reaction. In any case, this is very embarrassing situation for the CBS organization.

Although her comments were extreme, they were in the spirit of progressive thought. The DNC and progressive politicians immediately used the Las Vegas situation to push gun control ideology and to fundraise. Progressives never want to miss an opportunity to bulldoze their agenda forward and raise money no matter how inappropriate.

Anyone associated with Trump is fair game for news distortion by my local newspaper. For instance, a headline on an AP syndicated news story read "Tillerson in focus as Exxon investigation intensifies". The subheading read "New York AG looking into potential investor fraud". There was a picture of Tillerson with a caption stating he was under scrutiny for ExxonMobil misleading investors about the impact of climate change.

Buried within the news article was a single comment that said several republican state prosecutors from across the country have accused this New York attorney general of abusing the power of his office to score political points with his political base. The article was obviously meant to cast doubt on the integrity of our Secretary of State and the Trump administration.

A news story regarding the Russian meeting with Trump Jr., Manafort, and Kushner was in my local newspaper four days later. The headline said "Putin pal set up Trump Jr. meeting with Russia lawyer". That headline sounds very devious and supports the Russian collusion narrative but the article itself was very detailed about the nature of the meeting and made the meeting sound totally innocuous. There was no direct connection in the article between the person who set up the meeting and Putin. The newspaper editor who wrote the headline certainly did not want to be confused with the facts of the story.

There were two other articles, in addition to the one on the Russian meeting, that were very progressive and totally misleading regarding the truth. The headline on one of them read "State of hate in America escalates". The subheading was "In a deeply divided nation, incidents appear on the rise, growing more brutal". The article quoted research by SPLC, the Anti-Defamation League, and ProPublica—three very progressive social justice organizations. The article was 100% progressive propaganda used to bash Trump and support social justice.

The Washington Free Beacon reported in August that SPLC has $328 million in assets and received $50 million in donations in 2015. I find that very interesting but the most interesting comment in the article was that SPLC has reportedly transferred millions of dollars from past donations to offshore accounts in the Cayman Islands, British Virgin Islands, and Bermuda.

Why would a not-for-profit organization transfer millions of dollars to offshore accounts since there is not an issue of taxation? You can let your mind run rampant as I did. I saw millions of dollars hidden from public view in order to distribute that money to progressive organizations without public knowledge. I can see Antifa, Black Lives Matter, George Soros' Open Society, political campaigns, and others. How many progressive organizations could be doing the same thing? I have no proof—just thinking out loud.

Nothing was mentioned in the article about progressive individuals and progressive organizations that are the true cause of the increasing hate in America. The article included a picture of a group of young people who were labeled as members of the Ku Klux Klan. The Ku Klux Klan is on the verge of extinction and no longer carries out radical violence as it once did but it fits the social justice narrative. Why didn't they use a picture of the radical hate-filled violent Antifa organization? Because, Antifa is part of the progressive social justice movement. This was not a news article. It was a propaganda-laced opinion piece.

The third article was also a propaganda opinion piece disguised as a news story. The headline was "Europe's terrorist attacks show a surprising trend". What was the surprising trend? The subheading read "Killings peaked 4 decades ago when attackers were spurred by politics". The story said terrorism was worse in Western Europe in the 1970s, 1980s, and early 1990s when terrorists were political fanatics or agents of state-sponsored attacks like those of Northern Ireland's Republican Army.

The article quoted the European Union's counter terrorism director as saying it was difficult to understand why people become terrorists, whether their cause is religious or political. He blamed poor integration, poor education, discrimination, difficult neighborhoods, and the need to be part of a group and have purpose. I agree with him to a point but he left out the most important influence on today's terrorists—religious indoctrination to support jihad against all non-believers. Non-believers include anyone who is not a devout Muslim. He needs to read my original book, especially chapter 9.

The article also quoted a so-called security expert from a Brazilian think tank who said:

> Our societies in North America and Western Europe have managed over the course of the last century to reduce the risks of a wide range of factors commonly associated with death, ranging from various forms of acute respiratory illness and cancer to heart disease all the way down to car accidents and homicides. We know earthquakes and floods kill far more people than terrorism, but we give a huge amount of attention to terrorism even when it involves small numbers of casualties. It whips our society, which is a low-risk society, into a kind of frenzy and augments the perceived risk.

This quote is so bizarre that I had to sit for a minute after I read it in order to regain my wits. Then, I realized the quote supports an extremely important point that was made in chapter 2. Liberal idealism and liberal unconscious denial of unintended adverse consequences can enable society's destruction from within. Classic liberalism is too often idealistic and theoretical. Classic liberals believe that eventually their desired goals can be reached if enough time is allowed and sufficient effort is expended. Conservatism shares many of the same ideological goals as liberalism but conservatism is pragmatic, adjusts to fit reality, and reacts accordingly.

President Trump said the following during his September speech at the United Nations General Assembly, "We are guided by outcomes, not ideology." Gerald Seib responded to Trumps' comments with the following in a Wall Street Journal editorial, "In many ways, in fact, his address marked the return of U.S. foreign policy to realpolitik: a set of principles and precepts based upon practical considerations rather than philosophical or moral calculations."

I am always amazed that classic liberals fall in line behind radical progressives and their Marxist movement when, in reality, progressivism is a ruse and a contradiction to the basic liberal beliefs of equality and fairness. I see this phenomenon every day as I read letters to the editor in the Editorial Opinion section of my newspaper. These letters are based upon liberal thinking where emotion replaces fact and reason—well-meaning people off to the Milky Way searching for utopia.

Liberalism can be blinding and subject devoted followers to self-destruction by manipulative progressive elitists who, in their megalomaniac thirst for power and control, have the ability to destroy our American society. I am stunned regarding the extent these progressive elitists have manipulated well meaning liberals to follow them in their quest. Unfortunately, their destruction of American society will take the rest of us with them.

I read a quote that is appropriate for classic liberal followers of progressive ideology. Paul Simon of Simon and Garfunkel wrote the following line in their song titled *The Sounds of Silence*: "People hearing without listening". In contrast, conservatives are not perfect but are routinely grounded in truth and facts and do live in the real world.

Here is one of the best analogies I have ever read on this topic. It is by Cal Thomas:

There is one central characteristic to liberalism and it goes like this: No matter how many times an idea has been proved incorrect, or a program has failed to produce promised results, liberals still continue to believe in the rightness, even righteousness, of their cause. It is a cult-like faith that says something must be true simply because they and their like-minded colleagues believe it to be true. It's like Linus in the pumpkin patch. Each October the "Peanuts" character has faith that the Great Pumpkin will rise from among those other orange spheres and deliver presents. When he doesn't, Linus is disappointed, sometimes blaming himself for not having enough faith, but he remains undeterred.

So, what does this all mean and how does it affect the opinion I expressed in chapter 13 regarding the future of America? I said the question is not do we win or lose the battle to save our country but how fast we lose the battle. I gave the time period as being sometime during the next five decades depending upon future national elections. I based that opinion upon our society's current inadequate resistance and pushback to effectively stop the progressive onslaught on traditional America and the inherent mindset of our Millennial society and the leaders of America they produce.

I have revised my opinion based upon what I have observed and learned in writing this Epilogue after Trump was elected president. Trump's conservative based presidency has exposed how far Marxist-based progressivism has penetrated into our society and our government. When I wrote the original book I did not realize how pervasive this had become. I now believe it will not be a matter of decades to learn the future of America. America will take a dramatic left or right turn depending upon the Trump administration's and the Republican Party's success or failure in securing and maintaining conservative control of the country.

A left turn will mean progressive control of traditional America in perpetuity. They will take the country too far into Marxist

Progressiveland for us to ever recover. A right turn will take us back to my original opinion in chapter 13 unless our American society decides to wake up and emphatically tell the progressives to take their Marxist ideology and "stick it". It makes me sad to say it but I do not think that is likely based upon where society is today and where it appears to be headed in the future.

Obama and his progressive friends truly did fundamentally change America. They let the proverbial genie out of the bottle (a progressive genie, that is) and we are on the precipice of no return. IdiomCenter.com defines releasing the genie as, "Allowing something bad or unwanted to happen which cannot be stopped; to do something that causes a situation to change, so that it is no longer possible to go back to an earlier state." I hope and pray that definition is a false one for American society; however, I have increasingly become concerned as I observe how diabolical the progressives have been during Trump's presidency and are getting away with it.

Trump is doing a great job of reinstating conservative ideology in the way our federal government operates. The Republican Party; however, is weak in publicly fighting democrats and supporting Trump to preserve traditional American values. I saw side-by-side news stories in my local newspaper that paint a telling picture of how the democrats consistently malign republicans in Washington and the republicans sit back and take it. One article's headline said "Dems plan to force GOP votes to defend Trump". Pelosi was quoted in the article as saying democrats will begin to sponsor "resolutions of inquiry" to go after information on President Trump to use as "political fodder" in next year's midterm elections. She also said, "We will expose House Republicans' inaction, with their willful, shameful enabling. They have become enablers of the violation of our Constitution that attack on the integrity of our elections [*sic*], the security of our country. The integrity of our democracy is at stake. House Republicans will have to answer for their actions."

The headline of the news article next to the Pelosi article said "House (republicans) may modernize out-of-date dress code". The democrats appear to be concerned about securing the future of our country while the republicans appear to only worry about the dress code in the Speaker's Lobby off the House Chamber.

Pelosi's comments are classic progressive BS but that is what many Americans believe because they do not hear any strong counter from republicans. I will give republicans the fact that the mainstream news media gives Trump zero credit for his accomplishments, is biased against republicans, and pushes progressive BS but that does not excuse republicans for their lack of aggressive pushback against the democrats' constant false narratives.

I observe on television, read in newspapers, and see on the Internet the progressive democrats beating up the republicans on a daily basis and getting away with it. A great example is the tax reform bill. All the public has heard is the democrats saying the bill benefits the wealthy and hurts the middle class. Polls show the majority of Americans believe that is true. Where is the republican backbone and strong-will to publicly and effectively fight back with the truth?

With the unwavering support of the un-news media, Americans constantly hear how bad the republicans and conservative policies are and rarely hear the reality of how the democrats and their progressive policies are taking the country down the road of disaster. Messaging to the public is a huge problem with congressional republicans. Due to the progressives' tenacity, deceit, and news media support; they have a strong upper hand in political messaging. Hollywood and the television industry are also valuable allies in progressive political messaging.

How could a Marxist-based ideology that is so vastly contrary to our traditional American values become so strong in our country? It goes back to what I discussed throughout the original book and summarized in chapter 13. The American population has grown exponentially much larger and diverse during the last 241 years resulting in a more complex society and a significant percentage of individuals who are disenfranchised from our traditional society norms. I discussed in the original book the following issues that have created this disenfranchisement: the mobility and changing mores of society; the breakdown of the family unit; the denigration of religion; and a spoiled society based upon entitlement versus achievement resulting from our country's enormous success.

I read a very good article in Townhall by conservative blogger and columnist John Hawkins. Here is a very sobering closing paragraph from the article:

> There are still a lot of good people in this country, but as a nation, we've become complacent, decadent and jaded. We're the trust fund kid living off the money great, great-grandad left us while the family business we don't understand fails. What we have in America? It's rare. Historically, there are not a lot of extremely prosperous, free nations that don't have to fear invasion because of that powerful military. That means we are squandering an inheritance left to us by previous generations of Americans that we may never have again once it's lost. We foolishly assume it will be this good forever even though we laugh at and impugn many of the ideas, attitudes and principles that were responsible for our success in the first place. America is not on track for a happy ending and as much as I hate to say it, we're going to richly deserve the pain, misery and disaster our own actions are going to bring down on our heads one day.

I discussed in chapters 7, 8, and 13 the attitudes and actions of the future leaders of America—the Millennials. What was their reaction to Trump's election? I wrote the following in the first Epilogue regarding their reaction. There was open anger, disbelief, grief, and irrational criticism by a preponderance of these young people. There were demonstrations from coast to coast. I am sure many of those were by radical groups who protest anything they can find to protest and some were protesters like those we discussed who were paid to physically attack Trump supporters at Trump rallies. The rest of the protesters were naive and misguided young people.

One of the most immature actions was by the millennial who played

Aaron Burr in *Hamilton*. The play's writer and creator, who apparently is a progressive activist, in all likelihood orchestrated his actions. The millennial verbally attacked Mike Pence after the play was over as the then vice president-elect was leaving the theater. The *Hamilton* cast held hands across the stage and the actor preached to Pence, "We, sir, we are the diverse America who are alarmed and anxious that your new administration will not protect us, our planet, our children, our parents, or defend us and uphold our inalienable rights. We truly hope that this show has inspired you to uphold our American values and to work on behalf of us."

A significant number of young people in the audience booed Pence and cheered the actor on. I talked in chapter 13 about the millennial interviewed by Fox News' Jesse Watters who was going to see *Hamilton* because it was a popular play and had no clue who Hamilton was. I said it was amazing but not surprising how politically progressive these young people are and how totally clueless they are regarding the consequences of their ideology in the real world. Who are the true bigots in this scenario? Especially, considering the play's posted casting call said, "NON-WHITE men and women, ages 20s to 30s." This was one of the most egregious acts of bigotry, hypocrisy, rudeness, and disrespect I have ever seen.

Colleges, universities, and even high schools across the country coddled students to help them get over their "grief". Professors at many colleges and universities cancelled classes and exams to help students deal with their "Trump trauma". Thousands of high school students in several cities walked out of their schools to protest the election without any consequence.

In my day, we would have been suspended from school for that behavior. How are our young people ever going to grow up to responsible adulthood? They're not! I worry about what is going to happen when these young people become the bulk of American society and are forced to face reality. They have no clue regarding the struggles endured and sacrifices made by individual Americans and America as a country in order to give them what they have today. This cluelessness gives elitist

Marxist progressives the ability to exercise control over them with historical misinformation and utopian promises.

One of the more recent disturbing incidents took place at Southern Methodist University. The university is moving all lawn memorials to a place on campus cited by students as a "less prominent campus location" to protect students from what the university called "harmful or triggering" messages. One of the monuments to be moved is a 9/11 memorial. The governor of Texas objected to no avail. The manipulation of our young people by progressives is effective and very troubling as I discussed at length in chapter 10. Every time I write about these events, sadness comes over me as a blue blood American.

The Victims of Communism Memorial Foundation (VCMF) released a report this year titled "U.S. Attitudes Towards Socialism". The report showed that only 42% of Millennials viewed capitalism "favorably" while only 37 % had a "very unfavorable" view of communism. One-third of Millennials believed that more people were killed under Bush's presidency than under Stalin's reign. I discussed in chapter 10 that an estimated 62 million Russian citizens were killed under Stalin and his communist government. I'm still searching to find out who Bush killed. Forty-five percent of young people between 16 and 20 years old said they would vote for a socialist and twenty-one percent said they would vote for a communist.

Only 42% viewed capitalism favorably and more than half (yes, more than half) felt capitalism works against them. Forty percent believed the tax system should be changed so that the highest earners "pay their fair share" in taxes. Who do they think pay the taxes now? Remember, almost one-half of the population pays no taxes and the top 20% of earners pay about 85% of all taxes. That Kool-Aid must taste awfully good and, as I discussed throughout the original book, our young people are being fed more Kool-Aid every day by our educational system, the news media, the entertainment industry, and progressive politicians.

The Pickles cartoon characters, Earl and Opal, said it well in a recent cartoon. Earl said, "What happened in here? There's water all over the floor!" Opel responded, "The toilet overflowed, your grandson used too much toilet paper." Earl then said, "Well, I guess its like you always say to me … common sense is a flower that doesn't grow in everyone's garden."

Why doesn't common sense and reality grow in our young generation's garden as they mature? The following adverse influences on our young people were discussed in chapters 7, 8, 10, and 13: the breakdown of the family unit; geographic mobility; an attitude of "want and get" versus "want, strive, and get"; the diminished role of religion; moral decay; the electronic age; and the progressive takeover of our educational system.

This is not an optimistic picture for eradicating Marxist-based progressive ideology from dominance in our society in the long term, as these young people become America's leaders and the country's dominant voting block. The traditional American values that provide Americans the most personal opportunity, the most personal freedom, the best standard of living, and the best personal safety in the entire world are increasingly fading from our young society.

Mark Zuckerberg recently suggested a universal minimum wage for every American as a cushion to try new things. How does he think the U.S. became such an incubator for successful new ideas and products during the past two and one-half centuries? It was and continues to be the pioneer spirit, personal will, and opportunity to succeed in a free and opportunistic world that is afforded to all individual Americans. Did Zuckerburg get a universal minimum wage when he co-founded Facebook?

Zuckerberg has another great idea for Millennials. It has been reported that 36% of Millennials do not have any church affiliation and Facebook now has over 2 billion users. Zuckerberg has suggested that social media (Facebook) can provide the "community" that churches once filled as church membership drops. This kind of thought only exacerbates the issues discussed in chapter 13 regarding the breakup of the family unit and the de-socialization of our society. The following is a great quote on this subject that has been attributed to and not attributed to Albert Einstein: "I fear the day that technology will surpass our human interaction. The world will have a generation of idiots."

In chapter 10, I discussed the increasing progressive brainwashing of Millennials and subsequent generations through our educational system. Our colleges are also increasingly distorting and denigrating traditional American values. Colleges should be a "maturation incubator" for young adults—not a "baby crib" and an "anti-American incubator". Harvard President Drew Faust said the following regarding conservative speech on campus during Harvard's last commencement address, "We can see here at Harvard how our inattentiveness to the power and appeal of conservative voices left much of our community astonished, blindsided by the outcome of last fall's election. We need to hear those hateful ideas so our society is fully equipped to oppose and defeat them." That is an unbelievable comment by a university president, especially from the leader of one of our more renowned universities in America.

You probably remember that 100 plus students walked out on Vice President Pence's commencement speech at Notre Dame University. I heard a popular millennial co-host on a Fox News show comment that the students' actions were OK because they walked out "respectfully". What??? How can you intentionally walk out on someone when they are speaking, especially the Vice President of the United States, and not be disrespectful? That comment speaks for itself regarding millennial attitudes on civility and respect.

I read that socially minded companies are now giving social justice paid time off to allow their employees to protest. It has been my observation that these companies are predominately managed by and employee Millennials. I also read that Patagonia pays bail for employees who are arrested while peacefully demonstrating for environmental or related issues and will give time off for court appearances and legal appointments related to the arrest. This is absurd. Where is personal responsibility, personal accountability, and respect for the law?

Here is a story that is a great example of how members of our younger generation do not have personal understanding or appreciation of how well they have it today as opposed to generations before them. It was discussed in chapter 9 that the actions taken by Obama to change U.S. policy toward Cuba provided economic support to the Castro brothers and the Castro government versus the Cuban people and ignored Cuban human rights abuses.

When Fidel Castro died last year, Forbes estimated his net worth to be $900 million. This type of wealth is classic for totalitarian leaders of countries that are Marxist-based. I said in chapter 10 that the average salary in Cuba is $20 per month and my physician friend made $25 per month. Cuban citizens are entitled to a range of free services and subsidies—but!!! Marxist leaders like Castro always hide the wealth they accumulate on the backs of those they govern. It's a great example of the fallacy and hypocrisy of Marxist ideology that the progressives want to implement in America. I wonder what the total accumulation of wealth would have been for Hillary had she been elected. I often wonder about Obama's wealth and what we do not know. Are there foreign bank accounts we should know about? Sorry, I got carried away in thought. Back to my story.

The old guard Cubans in both Cuba and the U.S. said the Castro brothers manipulated Obama and Obama's actions were an affront against the Cuban people. They were very supportive of Trump reversing what Obama did. Millennials in Cuba and Cuban-American Millennials in the U.S. supported Obama's actions because they said it "might" open up new opportunities for them and they were opposed to Trump reversing the Obama policies.

The older generation remembers the hardships they and their families endured in Cuba under Castro's communist government until they escaped to America. The younger generation does not have an appreciation of what older generations went through. Here is an actual experience. I talked to the owner of my favorite Cuban restaurant who told me, with tears in his eyes, how lucky he was to be put on an airplane when he was 14 years old by his parents (without his parents, I might add) to have a better life in America. This was part of Operation Peter Pan, created by Father Bryan O. Walsh of the Catholic Welfare Bureau, in which 14,000 unaccompanied minors came to the U.S. between 1960 and 1962 to escape Castro's communism.

I also have a personal friend who was born in Cuba who told me how his family left everything behind in Cuba and came to America after his father served time in a Cuban prison. Human atrocities are not any better in Cuba today than they were then.

Even though these stories took place over 50 years ago, similar stories are abundant today throughout the planet and serve as examples of life in the real world outside our incredible country. Here is a great quote by English actor and producer Damian Lewis, "It's sad that children don't spend enough time looking around and being amazed by what's in the real world." That is especially true for our Millennials.

Our millennial population has no clue how good they have it and progressives make every effort to keep it that way in order to increase their power and control over them. No wonder our colleges and universities need safe zones on campus to shelter these young people from real life. The real world is waiting and progressive ideology will only falsely protect them to a point. The big question is who or what is going to protect them from the progressives when they reach that point? Remember that twenty-one percent of Millennials in America between 16 and 20 years old said in the VCMF survey they would support communism—totally clueless and very vulnerable.

Cal Thomas recently wrote a great op-ed that is pertinent to this topic. He said:

> When one has lost a standard for judging right from wrong, good from evil, when anything goes, then socialism and communism become one more organizing principle among many of equal value. ... We used to learn from the successful, because they served as role models and examples of how hard work and risk-taking could improve any life. Now we penalize success and, as a result, get less of it. But we feel better and feelings are all that matter, right? At least that's how we have been conditioned to think. ... Maybe a field trip to a communist country would cure Millennials of their moral equivalence. They might start by visiting the prisons in Cuba.

Progressives are succeeding in deceptively corrupting our history and destroying our traditional American culture. I discussed this issue extensively in chapter 10 and elsewhere in the original book. This past May, prior to the Charlottesville incident, Confederate monuments in New Orleans were taken down because they "celebrated racism". The monuments included a large statue of General Robert E. Lee. After the Charlottesville incident, it became a national movement by progressives to remove Confederate monuments anywhere they exist. It was an enormous overreaction to what happened in Charlottesville. Why would they do that? Wasn't it progressive Chicago mayor Rahm Emanuel who said, "Never let a good crisis go to waste."

An out of control crowd in Durham, N.C. toppled one of Lee's statutes after the Charlottesville incident. What the crowd did was against the law. The Durham County Sheriff said they would prosecute the vandals. That is really interesting since the police stood by and watched it happen. They arrested three people and said they were trying to identify others. One of those arrested was a young black female who climbed up the statue and put the rope around it to pull it down. She was identified as a member of a communist organization. Her association with communism is very telling and not surprising.

A Rasmussen pole taken in May showed 69% of Americans oppose efforts to remove these statues, 19% support them, and 12% are undecided. A Marist poll that was released after the Charlottesville violence surveyed what percent of American voters believed Confederate statues should remain as historical symbols: 62% said yes; 27% said no; and 11% were unsure. Republicans were: 86% yes; 6% no; and 8% undecided. Democrats were: 44% yes; 47% no; and 9% undecided. Independents were: 61% yes; 27% no; and 12% undecided.

If these polls are even close to being accurate in reflecting the beliefs of the American public, why is there such a loud effort to tear the statues down? The answer goes back to what I said earlier. During Obama's eight years as president, America was fundamentally pushed much farther to the radical left than most Americans realize. I pointed out in chapter 10 that Obama and his wife, Michelle, repeatedly chastised the white race with false information and accusations. Where was the outcry against Obama's racial dishonesty that Trump now gets when he accurately tells the truth regarding racial issues? We have already provided answers to that question but let's look further.

Here are some excerpts taken from articles written by Jack Kerwick in Townhall and Matt Walsh in theblaze. Kerwick said the following, "…the movement to remove all remnants of the Confederacy is a campaign against the West. It is a campaign against the European heritage of Western peoples. … The logic of the crusade to demonize Confederate heroes points inescapably toward the cleansing from the Western world of *all* white figures from our past who fail to satisfy the left's contemporary 'progressive' litmus test. …Winston Churchill said that 'Lee was the noblest American who had ever lived' … President Reagan described Lee as 'this southerner who criticized secession and called slavery a great moral wrong' and 'who would himself become an American legend'."

Walsh said, "First they tore down the Confederate monuments. Next they'll come for the Founders." His article pointed out that Lee never purchased a slave and freed the slaves he inherited from his wife's family before the end of the Civil War. Lee did not want to leave the Union. He was offered the command of the Northern army by President Lincoln but declined. He joined the Confederate army only after his home state of Virginia seceded. He did not want to march against his home and his family. He wanted to fight next to his sons and not against them. Kerwick made a very profound but troubling statement to close his article. He said, "A country that permits a magnificent man like Robert E. Lee to be demonized is a country that is on the road to ruin."

The biggest threat to the survival of America is Marxist-based progressivism. The second biggest threat, which is related to this progressive movement, is unchecked multiculturalism. It will destroy America if not brought under control and we demand those who want to live in America adopt and adhere to the laws and principles necessary to become legal U.S. citizens. Progressives claim that America was built on "multiculturalism". That is totally wrong. America was built as a "multiethnic" country with citizens who shared common desires, believed in the founding principles of our country, and supported those founding principles. America was not built as a multicultural society with conflicting ideology and principles.

The progressives are promoting multiculturalism to destroy our American society, as we know it. That gives them the power and control over us they desire. Assimilation is an enormous issue that is rarely talked about. The Daily Signal reported in March that almost 1 in 4 students in public schools across the country are from legal or illegal immigrant families. The article said this statistic raises "profound questions" about assimilation.

I read a June article in Townhall written by Victor Davis Hanson who is a columnist and expert in cultural and military history. He said, "The United States is currently the world's oldest democracy. But America is no more immune from collapse than were some of history's most stable and impressive consensual governments. Fifth-century Athens, Republican Rome, Renaissance Florence and Venice, and many of the elected governments of early 20th century Western European states eventually destroyed themselves, went bankrupt, or were overrun by invaders."

One only has to look back in history to learn that societies around the world have historically been in a constant state of flux. Civilized society only began a few thousand years ago. People began to settle down in 5000 BC, began to write in 3000 BC, and began to live by laws in 2000 BC. No society in existence today is the same society it was in its beginning.

Hanson said half the U.S. population, which is mostly liberal, is concentrated in 146 of our 3,000 counties. This geographic area is less than 10% of the total U.S. land mass and is located on the east and west coasts. The remaining landmass in the country's interior is mostly conservative and is geographically, culturally, economically, politically, and socially at odds with the liberal coasts. He continued that about 27% of Californians were not born in the U.S. and more than 40 million foreign-born immigrants currently live in the U.S.—the largest number in U.S. history.

This is interesting considering Trump would have won the popular vote by roughly 3 million votes if California and New York were excluded. This is in contrast to Hillary wining the popular vote by almost 3 million votes with California and New York included. The New York City and Los Angeles metropolitan areas are respectively number one and number two in the world with the highest percentage of foreign-born populations. These two areas of the country are progressive paradises for votes—especially illegal votes. Ask Hillary and her campaign staff! This is a very sobering analysis regarding the dangers of the uncontrolled cultural evolution that is taking place in America and is a great argument to keep the Electoral College and to address illegal voting.

Here is an interesting side issue. The Federation for American Immigration Reform (FAIR) recently released a report that said illegal immigration cost American taxpayers nearly $135 billion per year in federal, state, and local spending. We always hear from progressives that illegals pay taxes; therefore, they are not a financial burden on society and actually help pay the bills. FAIR estimated illegals pay $19 billion in taxes leaving a net cost to taxpayers of $115 billion.

It was discussed in chapter 8 that many families including illegals do not pay any taxes but get tax refunds (income redistribution) through tax credits. Not surprising the SPLC has labeled FAIR a hate group. I found it interesting that FAIR was founded by and is still controlled by individuals who are liberal. You can bet they are not progressive liberals.

Hanson said our country no longer adheres to its historical melting-pot assimilation and integration which will ultimately result in a fragmentation of society into "tribal clicks" that will vie for power, careers, and influence on the basis of ethnic solidarity rather than through assimilation and "shared Americanness". He said history has not been kind to "multicultural chaos". We only have to look at Europe today to see the enormous problems associated with the lack of assimilation; especially countries like Sweden, Germany, and England. The Swedish people have practically lost their country to Muslim immigrants and Muslim crime in Germany and England is increasingly becoming problematic.

Hanson predicted, "Either the United States will return to a shared single language and allegiance to a common and singular culture, or it will eventually descend into clannish violence." He gave California as an example and compared it to the Civil War, which occurred because southern states like South Carolina took the position that individual states were independent of and not bound to the federal government.

We have discussed that slavery was not the issue that caused the Civil War as repeatedly proclaimed by the progressives. It was states' rights. The Southern States that seceded and started the Civil War construed the Constitution to be a "compact" and not binding. Sound familiar? Look at the states and cities that are defying federal law today; i.e., sanctuary cities and states. Hanson said, "Read carefully what some prominent Californians are saying about the federal government: It is not much different from what influential Confederate South Carolinians boasted about in 1860 on the eve of secession."

The biggest threat regarding assimilation is Muslim immigration and Muslim refugees. Putting the terrorism issues aside, I have no problem with and encourage Muslims who want to become U.S. citizens and "integrate" into our society legally and completely to do so. I have an enormous problem with Muslims who come to the U.S. and refuse to fully integrate into American society. The Center for Security Policy (CSP) project that was discussed in chapter 9 found that 80% of the 100 Muslim mosques and facilities they studied in the U.S. preach anti-West extremism and exhibit a high level of sharia compliance and jihad threat.

Religious sermons in those mosques included the following language: women are inferior to men and can be beaten for disobedience; non-Muslims are infidels and inferior to Muslims; jihad or support for jihad is a Muslim's duty; suicide bombers and martyrs are worthy of the highest praise; and Islamic caliphate should one day encompass the United States. Doesn't sound very American to me.

A very recent event supports this attitude. The imam at the Islamic Center of Davis (California) posted a sermon on YouTube that called for the mass murder of all Jews. After a firestorm of criticism, the mosque issued a statement that said the imam was misunderstood. I read his comments and I wasn't confused. He said exactly what he was accused of saying.

CSP also did a study in 2015 that said 51% of the 600 Muslims surveyed declared Muslims should have the choice of being governed according to sharia law. We are already seeing isolated examples of this in certain parts of the country. This would be a disaster for American society if this practice were to proliferate. One only has to look at the contentious debates on television between Muslim leaders who live in the U.S. and have assimilated into American society and Muslim leaders who live in the U.S. and have no intent to assimilate. I have seen several of these debates on Fox News and the comments by those who refuse to assimilate are very alarming. The Muslims I watch condemning assimilation are not radical Muslim outliers. They are leaders in well-known Muslim organizations like the Muslim Brotherhood and CAIR.

Europe gives great insight into the enormous problems associated with the lack of Muslim assimilation into non-Muslim societies. In chapter 9, I talked about how the Swedish people have practically lost their country to Muslim immigrants who are increasingly exerting political clout and committing significant crime. I quoted Internet articles that referenced Sweden as the rape capital of the world.

Muslim Grooming Gangs are sex slavery organizations that seek out non-Muslim young girls for prostitution. They have proliferated in Northern England and are found in other European countries. They have also been found in the U.S. No-go zones are becoming increasingly more common in many European countries, especially in England and France. They are now also found in the U.S.

I have read about increasing unrest in Holland, Norway, and Belgium as Muslim immigration proliferates in those countries. Anywhere Muslim immigration occurs, significant problems result because of the lack of assimilation and major differences in societal values between the Muslim culture and those of the host country.

When one puts the following together: a spoiled society; a nation increasingly controlled by progressive elitists; a nation governed by ideological bias versus a nation governed by the people through Constitutional law; and a nation losing its hereditary identity—you have a nation that has lost its way and subject to self destruction. How close are we? We are getting pretty damn close!!!

As I write this, I am reminded of World War II. Love of country was so powerful during this very difficult time. Americans pulled together as one and did what had to be done to proudly defend their country and preserve freedom in the world, even considering the extreme hardships they endured on the battlefield and at home. America was a homogenous society committed to traditional American values. Because of our changing societal cultural values, the progressive onslaught against our traditional political ideological values, and the increasing problem of assimilation in our society; World War II would be a very different and very disheartening situation today.

I saw a documentary on the National Geographic television channel that depicted how the United States saved European countries from Russian led communist control after World War II. This was accomplished through financial assistance and providing food, supplies, and hope to Western European countries until they could recover. It was called the Marshall Plan and cost an astonishing $140 billion in today's dollars.

I watched film footage where proud Americans airlifted and personally handed out the food and supplies to the men, women, and children who were homeless and starving after the war's devastation. They provided hope through their kindness and caring persona while doing so. It was inspiring to watch such an outpouring of compassion and selflessness resulting from American patriotism. What do you think would happen today if a similar situation occurred like World War II? Would we see the American pride and personal loyalty to country that was present then?

Let's take a look at what the progressive movement will do to America if we can't put the progressive genie back in the bottle under the Trump administration. We are seeing what progressives are able to accomplish in Washington even when conservatives are in power. What happens if they gain back control of the White House? How about if they could also gain control of the House and the Senate? Progressives would increasingly manipulate liberals and minority segments of the population to maintain their support and votes. They would increasingly suppress the rights of the opposition by: verbal and physical intimidation through radical progressive organizations; onerous and controlling legislation; suppressing information regarding corrupt and anti-American government actions; coercion through government entities like the IRS and DOJ; suppression of free speech that is in opposition; indoctrinating our young people to Marxist ideology through education and other venues; and eventually brainwashing the entire adult population to endorse and support their Marxist ideology. We only have to look back at what happened during the Obama administration and imagine that behavior on steroids.

This sounds harsh and *1984*ish but look at the progress progressives made in eight short years. Look at how dysfunctional our society has become due to their efforts. Look at what the progressives are doing today to stop the Trump administration, conservative politicians, and the rest of us conservatives who believe in and push for traditional American values. George Orwell's son recently commented on his father's book saying, "His novel *1984* ... was really quite prescient ... Crickey, it's still fresh today as it was then."

I read an interesting article in The Daily Signal last May by Ricardo Pita, a law student and former Heritage Foundation Young Leader, whose family left Venezuela and moved to the U.S. when Chavez came into power. Here is an excerpt from his article:

> Socialism is a scam best understood by those who sell it and, eventually, the ones who abide by it. Over 20 years ago, under the banner of socialism and its endless list of impossible promises, demagogues hijacked Venezuela's government, dismantled civil society, and crippled the national economy. The socialists implemented measures that crippled the private sector and triggered massive capital fights and brain drain. Chavez's rise to power led to hostility toward journalists, persecution of political enemies, increased corruption, and higher crime levels. The gradual and continuing breakdown of the separation of powers meant the rule of law would further erode and the situation would grow more dire.

My parents left everything behind to give our family a second chance here in the U.S. This second chance allowed my brother and I to know and grow up in a country whose society is at its best when individuals are empowered, not burdened, by the government. This is a nation where civil society and strong families are the driving force of its natural vitality—where hard work is rewarded and success is praised. History has repeatedly shown socialism to be a corrupt and destructive force.

What powerful insight into a nation converted to Marxist rule that has the world's largest known oil reserves and its citizens do not have food to eat or basic supplies like toilet paper. Cruelty to Venezuelan citizens is also increasing at the hands of the Marxist government, which has become a communist totalitarian regime. Venezuela is an extreme situation; however, the Marxist principles and the outcome of those principles as articulated by Pita are the same principles and outcomes that my wife and I have observed around the world in Marxist-based countries that range from socialism to communism. I discussed many of our experiences in chapter 8.

America was more totalitarian under Obama than Americans believe or understand. We got much closer to what Venezuelans are experiencing than people realize. Think about how much power and control progressive politicians were gaining over us in Washington and in the states they controlled. If these progressives get back into the same position of power during the next elections, Americans will see a harder and faster push to take America to the point of no return under the guise of doing what is best for us. Never forget what Sunstein said in *The Nudge*.

With this dire but realistic prediction in mind, what do we Americans who love our country do? We do what I said in chapter 13. A quote by Cal Thomas explains it well. He said:

Let's employ a sports example. When a visiting baseball team is at bat, fans usually express themselves in loud voices hoping the batter will strike out. When the batter hits a home run and puts his team ahead, or wins the game, the crowd becomes quite. Success is also the easiest way to quell loud criticism in politics.

Here is a great personal example of Thomas' quote. Media Matters was going after Sean Hannity on Fox News to shut him down. This was after their success against Bill O'Reilly who had personal baggage they exploited. As you know, the progressives are continually trying to pick off Fox News personalities one by one to shut up conservative talk. I thought progressives were for free speech. Only, if that free speech is progressive speech. In the progressives' effort to get Hannity off the air, Media Matters (backed by George Soros) orchestrated a movement to contact Hannity advertisers and coerce them to cancel their advertising on his show.

My wife and I received an email from The Tea Party Patriots urging us to call two advertisers and support Hannity. We got a recording when we called Cars.com but our call to USAA insurance was a great success and proves Thomas' point. The very nice person who answered the call asked us what was going on? She said they had been getting numerous angry calls all day and many said they were canceling their insurance if Hannity was taken off Fox. We explained to her what was happening and she said she was sure we had nothing to worry about after what she had experienced that day. Hannity is still on Fox.

After I wrote the above, the progressives went after Hannity again. Hannity interviewed republican Senate candidate Roy Moore from Alabama after it was alleged he dated and sexually abused teenage girls when he was in his early thirties. Many pundits characterized the interview as Hannity being "tough" on Moore. I heard it and would agree. After the interview, Hannity commented, "Every single person in this country deserves the presumption of innocence. With the allegations against Judge Moore, none of us know the truth of what happened 30 years ago. The only people that would know are the people involved in this incident."

Media Matters again unleashed the progressive political machine to contact a number of Hannity's sponsors urging them to cease sponsoring Hannity's show because he "defended a child molester". That is totally not true. A few advertisers did cancel including Keurig coffee makers. Hannity supporters announced on the Internet they were going to boycott Keurig. Several supporters posted videos of themselves smashing their Keurig coffeemakers. Hannity said he was "humbled" and "laughing his ass off". He announced he was going to buy 500 coffee makers and give them to people with the best videos.

The CEO of Keurig wrote a letter to his employees and said, "I apologize for any negativity that you have experienced as a result of this situation and assure you we will learn and improve going forward." Don't think other advertisers didn't take notice as well. Standing up for traditional American values and aggressively pushing back against progressive behavior works and is the only way to stop them.

Unfortunately, those of us who believe in traditional American values are becoming less and less in number. A January Gallup poll indicated 36 % of the U.S. population identified as conservative and 25% identified as liberal. Since 1992, conservatives have varied between 36% and 40% of the population while liberals have increased from 17% to 25%. The increase in liberals came at the expense of moderates who dropped from 43% to 34%. Most of this change occurred after 2000 and Gallup said, "… the change was the result of one overarching factor—an increasing likelihood of democrats (including independents who lean democratic) to self-identify as liberal." Gallup said there has been an eight-point decline since 2001 in democrats identifying as conservative and a six-point decline in the percentage of democrats who identify as moderate.

Gallup did not have the advantage of my definitions of classic liberals and progressive liberals but I would assume that moderate and conservative democrats are classic liberals and liberal democrats are progressive liberals. Although disturbing, this trend is not surprising based upon the extensive analysis of liberalism in the original book and in this Epilogue.

What happens to those of us who oppose the progressives if we don't stop them before it is too late? The 1st Amendment of our Constitution guarantees freedom of speech. The 5th Amendment guarantees due process of law. And, our legal system is built on the principle of "presumption of innocence", which means one is considered innocent until proven guilty. Forget the protection of the Constitution and the law for those of us who oppose progressive ideology or get in the progressive's way. Progressives thrive on dystopian rule. If progressives gain the power to be in control of our country, they will parallel the Inner Party that ruled Oceania and will become the "Inner Party ruling America". Ponder that one!

It is past time for America to stand up strongly for America but I would first ask, "Does America know what it's standing up for?" Most Americans do not. Here are some disturbing statistics I found in one of Cal Thomas' op-eds. A poll taken by the University of Pennsylvania's Annenberg Public Center indicated that 37% could not name any of the five rights guaranteed by the 1st Amendment. Forty-eight percent did get freedom of speech. Only 19% knew the 1st Amendment guarantees freedom of religion. Townhall reported on the same survey and said only 26% of Americans could name the three branches of government. What happened to the required civics classes we had in school? Oh, the progressives got rid of them. That's certainly convenient.

Thomas said in his op-ed, "Ignorance about the documents that founded and have sustained America through many challenges ensures the country we have known will not be recognized by future generations. One can't have a country if its citizens are ignorant of its origins and purpose."

Here are similar quotes from our founding fathers:

- Benjamin Rush: Where there is no law, there is no liberty.
- Alexander Hamilton: If it be asked, what is the most sacred duty and the greatest source of our security in a Republic? The answer would be, an inviolable respect for the Constitution and Laws.
- Benjamin Franklin: A nation of well informed men who have been taught to know and prize the rights which God has given

them cannot be enslaved. It is in the region of ignorance that tyranny begins.

- John Adams: Liberty cannot be preserved without a general knowledge among the people.

The last two quotes are also found in chapter 6 expounding the dangers of the un-news media. We have repeatedly talked about the apathy in our country regarding the progressive movement and its increasing destruction of our traditional American values. Mallard Fillmore said it well in one of his recent cartoons. He said, "In a new poll, more than one in three Americans couldn't name any of our First Amendment rights. The way things are going, in a few years they may be right."

Earlier in the Epilogue, I shared my experiences regarding the three overwhelmingly patriotic Tea Party rallies in Naples where thousands of men, women, and children lined a busy street and peacefully protested Obama's progressive actions during his first months in office. I also shared the story of Glen Beck's Restoring Honor rally on the Lincoln Mall, which had hundreds of thousands patriotic Americans in attendance. There were many other rallies around the country as well. There was so much enthusiasm and pushback to defend our traditional American values by the thousands upon thousands of Americans who attended these rallies.

Where is the overwhelming enthusiasm to defend our way of life now? It makes me question more critically than ever any optimism I have toward America staying America. We discussed the modest expression of patriotic enthusiasm by patriotic Americans regarding the anti-American actions by the NFL. That does provide a glimmer of hope but the pushback against the NFL is nothing like the rallies in Naples, Washington, and other parts of the country eight years ago. Even the modest pushback against the NFL; however, had an effect. Advertisers felt threatened, fans turned on the teams, and television ratings dropped. Unfortunately, it wasn't strong enough to force the NFL to formally support American patriotism.

My hat is off to our president for saying any SOB playing in the

NFL who disrespects our country and our flag should be fired. One can say what they want about President Trump but he stood up to all the criticism he received including being called a racist. Trump is a champion for traditional American values and it is past time for American patriots who love our country to stand up with President Trump and support those values. We cannot rely on anyone else. It goes back to chapter 1 and Howard Beale. We, who love our country, must stand up and proclaim, "I'm mad as hell and I'm not going to take this anymore!" It is time to stand up with our voice and our actions and pushback when opportunities arise to put that progressive genie back in the bottle where it belongs. Lack of push back allows progressives to continue the destruction of traditional American values until those values are no more.

I do not condone violence or suggest it. We need to use non-violent ways to put violent and non-violent progressive demonstrators, progressive organizers, and progressive organizations in their place. There is a multitude of electronic and other means of communication to express opposition to the news media and others who promote progressive anti-American Marxist ideology. We need to also push back and demand accountability regarding the progressive nonsense that is taking place in our schools, colleges, and universities. We need to be in contact with our political representatives often and voice our opinions. Our pocketbooks are one of the loudest voices we have in selectively making purchases, watching only television and movies that do not push anti-American values, and making donations to organizations and politicians that love America as we do.

We have elections coming up in 2018 and our votes are the loudest voice we have. It is estimated that 250 million people are eligible to vote in America. Roughly 129 million voted in the last presidential election. That is only 52%. Where is the other 48%? Even though Trump won the electoral vote by 77 votes, Clinton won the popular vote by almost 3 million votes. That is the 5th time that has happened in our country's history. Americans need to get off their derrières and stand up for America as informed voters or accept America's demise from within.

Trump's campaign motto was "Make America Great Again".

President Trump and those in Congress who uphold traditional values cannot do it by themselves. This issue is bigger than them alone. The final outcome belongs to American society. The president and Congress are only able to kick the can down the road. Dinesh D'Souza said, "They can't take America from us without our consent." It will take a Howard Beale declaration by the majority of Americans—not just the 26% who voted for traditional American values in the past presidential election—to withhold that consent in perpetuity.

The original colonists came to America to escape religious persecution, escape repression, and to find better economic opportunity. If we lose America to the progressives and their Marxist-based ideology, we no longer have freedom of speech, freedom of religion, freedom from repression, or economic opportunity. Where do we traditional Americans who believe in the principles of our Declaration of Independence and our Constitution go? My wife and I have traveled in Central America, South America, Europe, Asia, and the Middle East. We have talked to many people who reside in those countries. We hear over and over how their countries are changing in a not so positive way—especially from the standpoint of opportunity for their children, economic success for their country, and personal freedom from government regulation and taxation.

President Trump eloquently summarized America's position in the world during his September United Nations speech. He said, "In America, we do not seek to impose our way of life on anyone, but rather to let it shine as an example for everyone to watch. In America, the people govern, the people rule and the people are sovereign."

There is no place to go and get back what we will lose if we lose our traditional American values to progressive Marxist rule because there is no place on earth like America—no place on Earth even comes close. When it's gone—it's gone!